What Teaching Means

Stories from America's Classrooms

D1369495

Edited by Daniel Boster and Marni Valerio

Rogue Faculty Press

Omaha, Nebraska

For teachers

and

their students

everywhere

❖ Contents ❖

Part Three: Realizing Potential

Part Four: Standing Up and Speaking Out

Part Five: Confronting Desperation

Part Six: Creating Connections

Postscript

❖ Preface ❖

What We Say We Love

Daniel Boster

In the fall of 1999, I was teaching English at Dominican High School in Whitefish Bay, a lakeside suburb to the north of Milwaukee, Wisconsin. It was my third year of teaching, and time for the fall open house. It is a private school, so, of course, recruiting is important. Open house was a time not only for current parents but also prospective students to visit the school. The administration teamed new teachers with veteran teachers. My partner was long time science teacher, Bernie Schreiner. Mr. Schreiner had taught there for over twenty years, and he was one of those teachers who had become a fixture of the school. He had outlasted several principals, gone through myriad "new" teaching methods, earned a meager amount of money for years, and said farewell to many, many graduating classes. Like many teachers who stick with it for a long time, he was a paradox. Perceived as grumpy, yet respected by his peers. Feared and loved by students. "Old school," yet innovative.

So, at open house, Mr. Schreiner and I were sitting in my classroom waiting for parents to arrive. I was tired from grading A.P. English essays about *The Stranger* and trying to figure out ways to help the struggling students in my "remedial" British literature course understand *Brave New World*. My wife, Marni, and I were in the process of buying our first home. The difficulties of balancing teaching and life were bearing down on me.

When parents weren't in the room, we talked about various things; Bernie mentioned that he preferred talking to students rather than their parents. We discussed the coming weekend's football games, the weather. Finally, our conversations turned to our shared students, the school itself, and teaching in general.

I was a little afraid of appearing foolish in front of him, so, for the most part, I kept quiet, listened, and nodded. Finally, near the end of the night as the hallways were clearing out, I asked a series of questions along the lines of: how had he taught for this long, at this school, when he could have made more money elsewhere? Why would a young teacher decide to keep doing this? He talked a bit about dedication, the fact that his kids went through school there, and the other typical reasons that a person stays in one job for a while. He trailed off. All that sounded pretty good, but I'd heard things like that from other veteran teachers. He got up and began gathering his things to leave, and I started to do the same. As he walked to the door, he turned around.

"I suppose that all sounds like bullshit to you."

I didn't know what to say. "Nah...O.K., sort of..."

"I can see that. Well, I guess I look at it like this. You love literature, right?" He pointed around the room. "You love talking about all these books."

"Sure."

"Well, Dan, you get paid, maybe not a lot, but you get paid to talk about what you say you love, every day. If you aren't lying, if you really love it, that seems to me like a pretty good deal. See you tomorrow."

I suppose some would hope that this short conversation turned into long term mentoring relationship like something out of one of those teacher movies that the public loves so much. You know...old conservative science teacher teams up with rookie liberal literature teacher to save the school from closing while partaking in witty banter and pulling off slightly rebellious acts to inspire students to rise above the odds of abusive or overbearing parents, to overcome drug use or gang violence, to cope with occasional rejection letters from Stanford, and so on. Didn't happen. Bernie and I never spoke of anything of consequence during the rest of my time at Dominican. I left the school, and Marni and I left Milwaukee after the next school year. He would likely be surprised at the impact of his words. He probably doesn't remember the conversation, and might even wonder why I do.

A dozen years later, I think about his words again. I have thought of them hundreds of times during my career, have repeated them to pre-service and young teachers I've worked with, have used them to make it through particularly tough days now and again. Lately, I've been thinking even more about why people do this work, what it means to be a teacher. I think that what Bernie Schreiner said to me that fall night in 1999 has a lot to do with it. Love, indeed, has a lot to do with this project.

***

The idea for this book started as one of those "wouldn't-it-be-cool-if" conversations that often happen when teachers are drinking coffee together. In the winter of 2011, I was troubled by disputes about public sector unions in Wisconsin, Ohio, Indiana, Nebraska, and other places, which led to the disparagement of teachers and teaching. Watching all of the news stories from state capitol buildings and the steps of schools all over the country last winter was upsetting but also inspiring. I heard a chorus of people calling teachers "lazy" and "greedy" and accusing teachers of "taking advantage of the system." All my experience told me these things weren't true. It suddenly seemed urgent that more people hear teachers' stories. I decided I wanted to know what was happening in the nation's classrooms.

A few months before, two of my colleagues, Jeff Lacey and Calvin Banks, had started their own publishing company, Rogue Faculty Press, to, in the words of their mission statement, "seek out projects that celebrate teachers whose talent might be ignored or overlooked." They believed that teachers' intellectual work deserved a home. They thought that they, as teachers themselves, would like to provide this home. Simply put, I believe more people need to hear about what teachers do each day, how our students and their experiences affect us, and how much we love what we do. So, with all of this in mind, I figured that someone should just ask teachers to tell their stories. Jeff and Calvin agreed to publish the result, and we got started.

***

I know I am biased, but I have always found most teachers (even before I was one) to be kind, funny, and interesting people. I wanted to be a teacher because I thought teachers seemed really cool and happy. I remember watching them talk and laugh in the hallways of my high school and how some of them would get these faraway stares while explaining *Hamlet*, Manifest Destiny, or polynomials. I thrived when I was around people who clearly loved what they were talking about and cared deeply about sharing that passion with their students. I even started wearing sweater vests in high school—and still do—because Mr. Hays, my favorite high school English teacher, did so on occasion. (I didn't realize at the time that sweater vests weren't really a hip look for a teenager.) The point is that I admired these people; I wanted to be like them.

My experience in a few different schools confirms my impression that most teachers are truly dedicated to teaching and their students. Naturally, like any profession, there are exceptions. Teachers aren't perfect. As is the case in any profession, there are a few people who don't do a good enough job. Some go into teaching for the wrong reasons. Of course, I hear all of the negative stories about teachers that seem to catch the public's attention. Too many of these stories are about predatory teachers who abuse their positions to manipulate young people. These stories sadden me deeply.

But, there are also stories of teachers doing great things that seem to go mostly unnoticed. I recently read that some teachers in Pennsylvania have agreed to work for free since the district ran out of money. Teachers, students, and parents discuss all of the positive things that happen in their schools every day. However, most really do care about their students and love, like Mr. Schreiner said, the ideas that they share each day.

I also believe that teachers and teaching are often misperceived. There seems to be a pretty simple reason for this: once they leave school, adults have very little interaction with teachers. People don't hear our stories. Most teachers love to talk about their craft, the growth of their students, and all the other cool things that happen in their schools, classrooms, and communities. However, most of the time, the only people who they tell about these things are other teachers. Thus, *What Teaching Means*. We wanted the stories—the funny ones, the sad ones, the inspiring ones, the strange ones—told and available to a wider audience.

***

Many people are struck by the fact that teachers' voices are often absent from the public dialogue about teaching and education. Politicians, corporate interests, and pundits tend to have the loudest voices, and they control those conversations. Again, there are reasons for this. Teachers' opinions aren't often solicited, and, when teachers do enter the political realm, the public often finds their involvement distasteful. While some educators make it a point to be involved in politics by working through local and national educators' associations, most teachers are simply too busy. Often, we don't have time to set aside our work as teachers to join the political fray. We don't hire our own lobbyists. Frankly, most of us would rather be in the classroom with our students.

But when teachers fail to tell their stories, something crucial is lost. Wisdom wrought from experience is neglected. Like most teachers, I read dozens of articles and books about teaching every year. I look for ways to improve my practice and better serve my students. I continue to go to school myself and am involved in conversations with teachers all over the country. I have learned a great deal from all of this, and I am a vastly better teacher for it. However, for the most part, I, too, am guilty of not speaking out enough. This entire project is an effort to allow teachers' voices to be heard.

This started as, and continues to be, a grassroots effort, and we are especially proud of that. News of the book spread by word of mouth, and we received stories from dozens of teachers in twenty-seven states. We heard from teachers in small towns, big cities, and everywhere in between. The submissions ran the gamut from kindergarten teachers to college professors, from retired teachers with forty years in the field to first year teachers, from principals to graduate students. Clearly, many educators felt the desire to share what they've realized about teaching. We asked teachers to tell stories that would illuminate their students' humanity and their own. We included many stories that do just that. However, we also heard from teachers both past and present, who were inspired to simply reflect on our core idea: what does teaching mean?

***

We believe that this book will speak to people who are considering teaching as a profession, those who feel the "calling" to teach. As I mentioned above, the stories in this collection chronicle a diverse set of experiences at different types of schools all over the country. We didn't want to pretend that all teachers tell their stories with one voice. These stories are as varied as the people and places they come from. A reader of this book will quickly realize that these authors don't necessarily only explore the great days in the lives of teachers and students. The teachers in these stories disappoint their students sometimes. They don't always say the right thing. They struggle with administrators and parents. They don't necessarily have all the answers. Some no longer even teach. In short, the stories are real. We don't pretend that they represent all the "best practices" or pedagogically perfect methods. More important to us is the recording of the deeply human stories playing out in schools everywhere.

Nonetheless, people who are considering being teachers can perhaps glimpse into what happens in our country's schools every day. There are a lot of people having a great time. There are stories of growth and death, new jobs and shuttered schools, blame and redemption. "Oh no" moments and "a-ha" moments. The quiet loneliness of not quite figuring it out and, finally, the lovely, and sometimes chaotic, noise of understanding. There are teachers who learn more than they can ever hope to teach, who receive more than they ever give. And, mostly, there are teachers who find a way to reach out to their students and embrace everything that teaching means, day after day, year after year.

***

Finally, I want to say a few things about the arrangement of the book. Unlike most books, we decided to include the authors' biographies with their stories. We did this because we believe that where teachers have taught, how they got to where they are now is crucial to understanding their stories. We hope that readers will see this collection as an invitation to think about their own stories, to explore what they think teaching means.

Teaching Means Learning from Students

The Escape Artist

Alicia McCauley

Brian was on the taller side. Well, as much on the taller side as you can be in first grade. He had downy blond hair and blue eyes. His smile was easy, and he'd not yet lost his first tooth. He came to me on the first day of school, shirttails tucked into pants pulled up way too high. He beamed when I commented on the gel in his hair and the shine of his new shoes. As I came to know Brian, it became apparent that he already struggled in reading and writing.

His kindergarten teacher noted that he was behind in language arts, but proficient in math and science. While most incoming first grade students could recall twenty or more letter sounds and read short words like "and," "the," and "can," Brian retained only twelve letter names, and, when he encountered the written word, he labored over each sound. While others were writing words and constructing basic sentences, Brian was penning strings of letters and random symbols. Brian and I began with the basics, spending time each day studying letter and sound correspondence.

By the time the leaves turned crunchy and brown, Brian had transformed into a functional reader and lover of writing. With help from a small literacy intervention group, he began to read simple, repetitive stories with multiple sentences on each page. During writing time, Brian used the words he'd mastered in reading to create stories of his own.

Each day, our class devoted time exclusively to writing. I'm not talking about handwriting practice, fill in the blank workbooks, or copying the teacher's writing. My students viewed themselves as authors with important things to say.

As a beginning teacher, I was clueless on how to teach writing, so I let my students select their topics and assisted and answered questions when needed. As students worked, I would stroll around the room, often pausing to read snippets of their writing. Despite my miniscule knowledge about teaching the craft of writing, my students bubbled with excitement at the opportunity to record their thoughts and, above all, staple together books of their very own stories.

Friday afternoons, my class would cluster on the carpet to read drafts of their own writing from the seat of the Author's Chair. The children on the carpet were rapt, as they listened to and applauded story after story. When a student would scoot down off the chair, a flurry of hands would shoot up. All were eager to be the next reader. Most of my students chose to leave their books in the safe haven of the classroom. Consequently, our classroom brimmed with their books. There were books sandwiched on the shelves, leaning in the windowsills, stacked in cubbies, spilling out of desks, overflowing out of book boxes, and, just when I thought we'd run out of space, we tacked their books up on the walls.

Brian took pleasure in writing about his family. He wrote about his mom, his grandma, his sister, and his rowdy hoard of cousins. His stories were predominantly retellings of exciting vacations to every place a kid could dream of visiting.

Several times that year I'd sent notes home and left phone messages to tell Brian's family about the tremendous progress he was making. My attempts to connect with his parents went unanswered, but hearing the stories about his close knit family set my mind at ease. Parents are busy. I understood. So, each Friday in the Author's Chair, Brian would sit up straight, clear his throat, and read his latest adventure with his family.

One day the principal asked me to escort Brian to the office during lunchtime. Brian was not a troublemaker; he befriended everyone and avoided conflict at all costs. Lost in conversation about his recess plans, we walked hand in hand up the hallway, oblivious to the police cruiser in the parking lot and the possibility that its presence was linked to Brian. As we stepped through the office doorway, my eyes met the gaze of a police officer. A child protective services caseworker stood beside her. My heart dropped like a stone. The caseworker spoke with Brian privately while the officer filled me in on the details. Brian's father was in prison, and his mother had just been arrested for possession of methamphetamine. According to the officer, this was an ongoing case, which included prior arrests and visits to the home.

Brian would be relocated to a foster home and a new school that very day. His little sister would be placed in a separate home. I was blindsided.

As he returned to the office with the caseworker, Brian cried from a deep and broken place. I rocked him like a baby, feebly assuring him that he would be loved in this new home and at his new school. He was adamant about returning to his mom.

"My mom is a *good* mom! My mom is a *good* mom! I want to go back to *my home!*" he wailed, sucking in his bottom lip and struggling for breath. After forty minutes of rocking, crying, and desperate screaming, Brian caught his breath and paused. "Can I do Author's Chair today even though it's not Friday?"

I was speechless. I would have wrapped the moon in a silver bow and placed it in his small hands had he asked.

When the lunch bell rang, the class sat at the carpet. Brian sat in the Author's Chair, straightened his back, cleared his throat, and through red-rimmed eyes began to read. He read about a trip his family had recently taken to Disneyland. I knew it wasn't true. He knew that I knew it wasn't true. In that moment, I knew that all of his stories about his family were false. Brian finished reading, and, with my heart in my throat, our class said our goodbyes. Our paths did not cross again.

On that tear-streaked day, it was starkly apparent to me that writing was a survival mechanism for Brian. Perhaps his stories were wishes he'd hoped would come true if he scratched them out on paper. I've always known that writing has the power to whisk an author away to unknown and exciting places, but what I learned from Brian is that writing can also sustain a person in places that are painfully real. His fictitious life created a safe space of normalcy. Pencil in hand, he scripted the life he both craved and deserved.

I often wonder what became of Brian. At night, between the hazy edges of dreams, I glimpse his face amongst other children who have come and gone too quickly. I regret not seeing beyond his eager smile and bright eyes. I regret not hearing Brian's real stories, the ones that were too hard to tell.

That day was a turning point in my life. It changed who I am as a person, who I am as a teacher. I pursued parents with regular phone calls, and, when they didn't call me back, I called them at work, flooded them with notes, and even dropped in on them at home. Shiny new shoes, freshly gelled hair, and parents who appeared "too busy" would never again lead me to assume a loving home existed for any of my students.

Most of my digging into their lives produced discoveries of yards littered with bikes, parents eager to hear about their child's school life, and, above all, families with deep love for their children. Occasionally, I uncovered a family without electricity, a kitchen with hollow-eyed cupboards, or a parent undone by addiction. Digging beyond the surface allowed me to see the real stories of my students, and I did my best to use the intimate knowledge of my students' lives to help them obtain whatever resources they needed.

Several years have crossed the calendar since my time with Brian, and not a day passes without his story rising to the surface of my mind. Questions about how I could have better served Brian became questions of how I could create a space for my current students to write honestly, even when honesty plumbed more painful depths. Over the years, my shock over Brian's abrupt departure gave way to grief. Grief was shoved aside by guilt. And guilt became my catalyst for change.

I recognize that some children have tumultuous lives outside of school. Lives that I cannot always understand. Lives that I cannot always change. The guilt I feel lies in this one lingering thought: if I'd given Brian access to words sturdy enough to bear the weight of his reality, maybe, just maybe, those words would have given him the courage to write the heartbreaking truth.

Yes, Brian demonstrated tidy handwriting. He applied correct sentence structure, but that was not enough. That is not enough. I wanted Brian to have the power, or at least the choice, to write honestly. While fiction can be a captivating vehicle, fiction under the guise of truth is hollow. Writing that comes straight from the heart is what I want my students to strive for.

Although I don't possess a word of Brian's writing, the lessons I learned from him serve as the foundation of how I teach young writers today. Brian confirmed my belief that young writers need daily writing time and ownership of their pieces, but the greater gift is that he continues to compel me to seek out opportunities for my students to write openly and honestly.

Still, there remains a tender place in my heart that pulses with sorrow because the lessons I learned were too costly for a six year old. Even for one on the taller side.

Alicia McCauley earned an A.A. in early childhood education from Shasta College, followed by a B.A. in liberal arts and a teaching credential from Simpson University. After receiving her teaching credential, Alicia began teaching first grade and hasn't looked back since. She teaches first grade at Boulder Creek School in Redding, Califonia. In addition to teaching, Alicia facilitates writing workshops for fellow teachers as a teacher consultant for the Northern California Writing Project. Alicia is married to her high school sweetheart and is busy living happily ever after. She blogs about her teaching life and life in general at: *www.pedalsandpencils.com.*

A Totem

Spencer Pforsich

I learned far more from Martin Graham than he ever learned from me. In my second year as a teacher, Martin was in my sophomore humanities class. He was born with a unique neurological disorder that gave him what his mom described as "mini-lighting storms in his brain." When they happened, they would disrupt his thoughts, his speech, and his movements in ways that were confusing and, sometimes, alarming to witness. Martin was also emotionally less mature than his peers, another result of his disorder.

Because ours was a project-based school where work was frequently done in groups, it was always a challenge finding students willing to work with Martin and figuring out how to fairly assess his contributions to a project. I can recall more than once when I had to step in to mediate for stressed-out fellow group members who had given up trying to talk to, reason with, or otherwise tolerate Martin. He was also terribly stubborn, which didn't help matters.

Of course, Martin was also so much more than these things. He was full of kindness, love, and compassion, and he was wholly incapable of understanding hatred or injustice. In class discussions about big ideas like genocide and slavery, it was always Martin who asked the question at the heart of everything: "Why are people so cruel to each other?" He was deeply passionate about art—a talent that reminded his peers that he was intelligent in spite of how his disabilities made him appear. Amazingly, he also rode a unicycle and performed whimsical tricks with a Chinese yo-yo.

Martin taught me to be infinitely more patient, flexible, and creative in my teaching. He taught his classmates to accept his idiosyncrasies, to see the world from his novel perspective, and to care about themselves and one another. Although I sometimes struggled to understand Martin, I had great respect and love for him. I wish I could have been there to witness his graduation in California last year, to see for myself an event that some of his family never expected would be possible. Now he's off to art school in Los Angeles, flourishing among kids just as kooky and out-of-the-box as he is. I still occasionally hear from him and his mom, and it always humbles me to know how much joy Martin brings to his world.

I think about Martin (and a few others like him) when I feel discouraged by my work. I carry him with me like a totem, reaching into my head and pulling him out when I feel like things are just too hard. Most teachers I know have a Martin Graham tucked in the pockets of their memories. Having these students in class is never convenient when it's actually happening since they require us to be better than we think we are. But these are the experiences we come back to again and again in our minds. They give us hope and inspiration when we feel like we have none. And they remind us, above all, that this is the greatest job in the world.

Spencer Pforsich received a B.A. from the University of California, San Diego. He received his M. Ed. from the High Tech High Graduate School of Education, the nation's only graduate school of education housed entirely within a K-12 institution. He has taught high school English and social studies in California and Wisconsin, and his passion for diversity education has led him to serve as faculty advisor for the Gay Straight Alliance and the Student Forum for Social Justice. In summer of 2011, he served as a teacher-leader in the inaugural cohort of the Greater Madison Writing Project. He currently teaches literature, writing, and is the yearbook advisor at McFarland High School in Madison, Wisconsin.

I Am Helen. You Are Annie.

Katie Schrodt

Imagine the scene. It is the first day of school, and *everyone* has the jitters...especially in kindergarten. One quick glance around the room, and you would see Mommy's crying, Daddy's grabbing the arms of the crying mommies, kids sheepishly staring at all the strangers in the room, me buzzing around trying to touch every kid and crying mom with a calming pat, little siblings terrorizing the bookshelves, and one office staff member warning me of a last minute deathly-allergic-to-peanut-butter-kid. The scene is wild and bustling with energy. After hanging up backpacks and learning cubby numbers, the kids finally settle down, and the parents hesitantly leave the classroom. The school year has begun.

We start each kindergarten year with a unit on the five senses. This unit is always a hit with the children as they experience their senses first hand through taste tests, temperature measurements, and "guess what's in the brown bag" touch tests. We use our ears to listen to heavy metal music and classical symphonies. We use our eyes to observe the beauty in nature. We use our noses to smell sweet cinnamon and stinging black pepper. But above all other things in this unit, we learn about Helen Keller and that always steals the show. This year was no exception. "Mrs. Schrodt, why can't Helen see?" "Mrs. Schrodt, you mean she couldn't hear anything?" "Mrs. Schrodt, she hit her own teacher?" "Mrs. Schrodt, why did Annie Sullivan love Helen?" "Mrs. Schrodt, is Helen still alive? How did she die?"

As a class, we answer every question a little five-year-old could come up with about Helen Keller. We read the story of Annie Sullivan and her journey to become Helen's teacher. We watch YouTube interviews with Helen Keller, and we even experience what it is like to lose your sight by being led blindfolded down the hallway by other kindergarten peers.

I always enjoy this time as a teacher. I watch light bulbs go on in their heads as many of them think about people with disabilities for the first time in their lives. They approach it with great child-like hope and compassion. This year was no different. Except this year, we had Stefanie.

Remember that chaotic scene on that first day of school? In a classroom full of unsure people, there was one picture of confidence. Cool as a cucumber, Stefanie struts into the room backwards, stops, turns, and announces, "There is a reason I am walking this way. This is a *brand new backpack, people,* and it should be the first thing you see in this class!" This little girl with the teasing sparkle in her eye, blunt-cut bangs, Dora the Explorer band aid across her nose, and thumb in her mouth…The phrase "marches to the beat of her own drum" is rarely so applicable.

Stefanie is the kind of student a teacher will remember forever—the kind that leaves a shoes-on-backwards footprint on your heart. But she isn't the typical straight A, straight-laced, teacher's-pet kind of kid in all the stereotypes. Oh no! She isn't even your "Fancy Nancy" type character that loves to be unique and girly. Stefanie is just Stefanie, and there is no other way to put it. The only problem is that she never liked to be called by *that* name. From day one, she insisted on a variation of names. There was Squirt, Sparkles, Texas-Cat, or Linus (because *he* sucked his thumb just like her). During the five senses unit, she insisted on being called "Helen."

It was towards the end of the unit, and Stefanie and I were struggling together over writing the letter S. Although Stefanie had the vocabulary of a teenager, she had spent all summer with a tutor trying to learn to write her name, to no avail. As Stefanie sat squirming in her desk laughing and throwing her head back, she said in an exasperated tone, "This is HAARRDD." The teacher-voice in my head began to think "Oh my goodness…it's only August…I have eight more months of this…this is HOPELESS." I tried to calm Stefanie down and continued to tell her she was fully capable of writing the letter S if she would just calm down and sit still for a second. Her hands shook with excitement as she popped up and down out of her chair giggling and glancing at me with hilarious eyes covered by disheveled hair that said, "Mrs. Schrodt, you KNOW I am not going to do this." And in the middle of one of those glances, suddenly Stefanie stopped. She was completely still for what seemed like an entire minute. Her eyes s-l-o-w-l-y made their way up my body and then locked in with mine. "You know what this is, right, Mrs. Schrodt?"

I looked at her confused. "What are you talking about, Stefanie?"

"This is *just* like Helen Keller and Annie Sullivan. I am Helen, and *you* are Annie. You are just trying and trying your hardest to teach me, but I am just *not* going to learn. In fact, from now on, you must call me Helen, and I will call you Annie."

For the rest of the five senses unit, Stefanie walked down the hallway with her eyes closed and one hand outstretched "feeling" her way around "just like Helen would" with the other thumb tucked in her mouth. She answered only to the name Helen and started up riveting games of "Helen and Annie" at recess. "I'll be Helen, and YOU be Annie," she would say adamantly to her friends.

This very moment was the moment I knew I had a genius on my hands. This was no ordinary kindergartener, even if she *did* struggle to write her own name. No! The depth of the connection she had made from Helen Keller to her own life was astounding. Stefanie didn't have me fooled each time she told me, "You KNOW I don't read or write, don't you, Mrs. Schrodt?" I knew that when she decided, she would not only write her name, but also go further than any kindergartener I've ever had. By making a connection a to Helen, Stefanie was quietly saying, *although I struggle now, I will succeed.*

And so Writer's Workshop began.

Our little classroom family began to notice, to wonder, to observe, to realize, and to hide all of our treasures in our writer's notebooks. We began sharing stories, talking about family vacations and soccer practice. We began laughing at the time we saw the smashed diaper in the parking lot when we were walking to the playground. We stopped and observed the Stick Bug that Solomon found hanging on a tree limb. We listened to the fears and hopes of our friends and shared our own dreams as well. We were being hemmed together as a class, and the thread was writing. These fragile five year olds were writing about everything from funerals of family members to their latest injuries to cooking with their moms to playing "Ninja" at recess.

And, as I knew it would happen since Stefanie "became" Helen, her heart and mind began to open like a blooming flower and spill out all over the page. It was almost as if overnight she went from the little girl who couldn't write the letter S to the flourishing young lady who wrote about how many "sleeps" until her dad got home from his business trip or about an "adorable" teddy bear her mom bought her last weekend. She poured over the pages stories about her sister waking her up during the night and wishful dreaming about one day having her own pet. But my most cherished stories were about her favorite chapter books she loved to read. *"Funny girl,"* I giggled in my head. *"She can't read chapter books."* But, as the days went on, I noticed a trend. Stefanie would round the corner of the kindergarten hall every morning on her way to my classroom with her hair going buck-wild and her pants on backwards or hanging off because she "had no hips" (or so she said). When she spotted me waiting at the door she would pull a chapter book right in front of her face as if she was reading. As she got closer, she would slowly pull the book down right below her eyes, just enough to say, "Hi Mrs. Schrodt. I'm reading *Last of the Mohicans*...chapter 5." Or "Hey Mrs. Schrodt. I've got this *Junie B. Jones* book...I read the whole thing last night." Or "Oh my goodness...this *Charlotte's Web* book sure is long." I would laugh to myself, but a voice in the back of my head began to wonder. Maybe she really *was* reading those books. I knew she was great at reading sight words, but she had never read a full book for me. Time went on and I dismissed the thought. But Stefanie and I continued to study each other.

One day at recess, Stefanie came to me and said, "Mrs. Schrodt, let's play that game where you are my owner, and I am your Texas-Cat. When anyone comes over to you say, "Shhh! My Texas-Cat is sleeping." And so we played the game. I must have said, "Shhh! My Texas-Cat is sleeping" about twenty times that recess.

Our bond was growing stronger.

Now lest you think all of this learning had stifled Stefanie's "Helen Keller" side...you are wrong! Stefanie *loved* to tease. And she especially loved to tease me. She said it best herself when she said, "Trust me, I *know* I would have eaten the fruit off that tree, juuuuust like Eve did." Stefanie did things differently! I used to try and encourage the kids by telling them that I was also a student and learner, since I am going to school to get my master's degree. One day I was telling them about how I went to school the night before. In the middle of my inspirational speech (or so I thought) Stefanie interrupted me with, "Mrs. Schrodt, you're *sooooo* annoying how you're always talking about 'how you go to school, too.'" Her finger quotes waved in the air at that last part. I looked at her somewhat baffled until I saw the look in her eyes. It was a look of pure love. Her thumb was in her mouth, but her eyes glistened with a smile, as if to say, "It's just me Mrs. Schrodt. You know I am just teasing you because I like you." So, I said back to her with a grin, "Ooohh, so that's how it is, huh?" And the whole class started laughing together. Stefanie and I shared a knowing look. We understood each other.

Our love was weaving tighter.

One brisk winter morning, I finally asked Stefanie to let me in on her chapter book secret. As she sat reading her C.S. Lewis classic I asked, "Hey Stef, will you read a little bit of your chapter book to me? I love *The Lion, The Witch, and The Wardrobe*! Don't you?" She looked at me suspiciously and shrugged her shoulders... *"Once there were four children whose names were Peter, Susan, Edmund, and Lucy. This story is about something that happened to them when they were sent away from London..."* As I listened to Stefanie continue to read, I felt my heart begin to fill up and overflow into tears in my eyes. This was the little girl who spent the whole summer trying to learn to write her name. This was the little girl who was being pulled out for individual tutoring. This was the little girl who tested the waters the entire fall semester to see if I could be trusted. She had found her voice. It had always been there, but she decided to let me in. She swung open the doors of her heart with wild abandon and showed me everything. Stefanie had dug down deep. She had planted a seed with that first connection to Helen Keller. She had watered that seed as she explored her own life through writing. She had poured sun onto that seed as she locked eyes with me and knew we understood each other. And with all of those things, a flower began to bloom.

And it is the most beautiful flower in the world.

On the last day of school, I pulled Stefanie close to my body and said, "I love you Stefanie. I am going to miss you so much! Thank you for being in my class."

And she looked at me and giggled and said, "Oh Mrs. Schrodt, you sure do know how to make a girl wanna cry."

So instead of crying, we spent our last minutes together laughing.

Katie Schrodt received a B.S. from the University of North Texas and is currently working on her M.Ed. in literacy at Middle Tennessee State University. Katie is a teacher consultant for the Middle Tennessee Writing Project and has a passion for teaching children to view themselves as writers who have a voice that matters. She has taught kindergarten and third grade in Texas and Tennessee. She currently works in Franklin, Tennessee, at New Hope Academy. New Hope Academy is a Christ-centered community school with an economically, racially, and culturally diverse student body that exists to serve low-income families in middle Tennessee. Due to the model of this school, Katie is able to teach and empower the whole child. She has implemented a writer's workshop model, as well as an after school ministry called Table Top. Katie lives in Nashville with her wonderful husband, Jacob.

Uncertainty

Mary G. Powell

"Hnhnn?" Beneath his mop of dirty blond hair, he grunted a muffled reply.

"Steven, I can't hear you. Why didn't you finish your homework?"

"Because we got home late," Steven looked me square in the eye, staring me down—Wyatt Earp and Doc Holiday rolled into one.

I was teaching ninth grade English, and, as a third year teacher, I was feeling a little lost. When I graduated from Arizona State University with my teaching credentials, I was set on fire, ready to take on the world. I wanted to teach at an urban, Title I school where I felt I could "better" the lives of my students and provide them with opportunities that they might not otherwise have. Little did I know that they would teach me a thing or two. For one, at least two of my girls over the past three years had babies, something I knew nothing about. Secondly, some of my kids came from homes where parents abused drugs, alcohol, and, sometimes, their children. My students had acquired the self-defense tools of a ninja while I had mastered the art of the metaphor and the simile.

"Steven, if you want to pass this class, you have to do your homework. No excuses! I know you can do it, and I want the best for you. Don't you want to go to off to college? Get a profession?"

"Is sleeping and drinking Slushies from Circle K a profession?"

Upon seeing my sour look, Steven muttered, "Then I would rather sleep."

So my students weren't the most motivated, but they were intelligent. Steven was the first of the Cook brothers who I would instruct. I eventually taught English to four of the siblings, two of which were identical twins. The oldest brother in the Cook clan earned a 1600 on his SATs and received a full-ride scholarship to attend a prestigious university on the East Coast. The Cook family consisted of seven siblings, with a single teacher-mother and one grandmother to raise them, in a three-bedroom apartment. The children had four different fathers; at least one of the dads was in prison. One of the boys went off to a fire science academy; two others were in honors classes at our school. But Steven, the second sibling was, I believe, tormented by his oldest brother's successes. And, when you can't be the golden child, sometimes you become the black sheep.

The bell rang for my second hour class to leave. Steven shuffled out of the room. He wore a black t-shirt, Dickies brand shorts, and worn out Nike shoes, unlaced, that shuffled against the cold linoleum.

***

For weeks, I tried to think of a way to reach Steven. On some days, Steven would turn in homework that exceeded the page limit. He composed an essay on *Moby Dick*, a reading of his own selection, analyzing syntax, diction, and covert metaphors—the stuff of graduate students. Other days, Steven would only write his name in microscopic penciled lettering, put his head down on his desk, and go to sleep.

On the most memorable of days, he was quite combative. We had started a debate on the death penalty in which I had required students to debate for the side that was opposite of their actual views. I placed Steven on the team that was in favor of the death penalty since he was animatedly against it. "The white man is responsible for all of this shit!" he exclaimed. (He is, in fact, white). "Why should men be punished when they are forced to live in a society that makes them act unjustly? Fight the power!" He raised his pale fist high into the air.

The class roared with laughter. During the debate, however, he was all about his side. He interrogated his peers, "So, we should just release murderers and thugs on the streets?" He boldly applied the facts that I had handed out for the activity, "According to page sixty-seven, the death penalty deterred crime in New York State by 58%. How can you not justify sentencing someone to their execution when they have murdered another human being?"

Steven worked the classroom like Perry Mason. At the end of class that day, I stopped Steven as I had done many times before. "Hey, you did a great job today."

"Yeah, whatever."

"No, you really did. You should consider being a lawyer," I smiled. I was setting Steven on the right track, helping him determine his future, allowing him to grow and become something in society.

"Hell *and* no!" He crossed his arms defiantly, his Public Enemy t-shirt a subtle backdrop to the gesture.

"Why not?"

"Why would I? Why take a meaningless exam, spend thousands of dollars on school, and spend taxpayers' money, so I can become a part of a totalitarian system that fights for one group of wealthy people while ignoring the rest? I would basically get paid to lie for my clients. What kind of shit is that?"

Steven stomped out. My mouth was agape.

That evening, while I was eating takeout Vietnamese food and listening to the monsoon rains of Phoenix patter upon my window, I pondered Steven's views. He had a point. What was I trying to achieve with my students? We had a fun debate; the kids learned how to use rhetoric, avoid faulty logic, and would, hopefully, pass their district exams. But what was I teaching them? I asked them to advocate for ideals that they didn't necessarily believe in. Was I corrupting their young minds? Was I merely perpetuating the status quo? In the fashion of a new teacher, I stayed up most of the night worried about how I was impacting my students. It's funny how much I worried about the influence I had over my students when there are so many decisions that they make on their own without the approval of the adults in their lives.

As fall turned to winter, the desert turned cold. The eighty-degree temperatures we had encountered in October turned to a chilly fifty degrees. One week, we had freeze warnings on the news, heard that citizens should cover their shrubs and trees to protect them from the cold morning frost. Steven always wore the same clothing regardless of the weather. Rain or shine, a black t-shirt, black Dickies shorts, and Nike sneakers—sometimes without of socks—were his battle attire. One morning, I asked Steven if he owned a jacket.

"No."

"Aren't you cold?"

"Naw; it's all up to a person's perspective."

"What do you mean?" I asked.

"If I make up my mind that I'm warm, I'm warm. I can choose to be cold and shelter myself from the world or be free and embrace what the environment brings me."

"But won't you get sick?"

"No. I never get sick."

Steven insisted that he was fine, but I felt differently. The motherly instincts in me led to a trip to Kmart that weekend. I scoured the aisles until I found the perfect piece of fashion for Steven—a black Dickies jacket.

On Monday morning, after class, I pulled Steven aside.

"Wassup?"

"Steven, I brought you something." I pulled the jacket out of the plastic bag and shyly presented it to him.

"What's this?"

"A jacket."

"Nope, I don't need a jacket. I already told you I don't wear them. I have nothing to hide."

"But I want you to be warm and…"

"No!"

Steven turned on his heel and left. I felt alone, saddened, sorry that I had purchased that coat. Different emotions washed over me, as I pondered all the things I should have said and done instead. I could have played the stern teacher: *You will not have that attitude with me! Apologize for that tone or I'm sending you to the dean.* Loving teacher: *Steven, please try it on. I don't want you to catch a cold.* Or better yet, cool teacher: *Whatevs. I found it in my closet, just thought it might match your digs.* It was just a jacket, so why did it bother me so much?

Three years later, Steven was placed in my twelfth grade honors English class. He dropped it after four weeks, with an F, saying it was too much work for him. His writing and reading skills still far exceeded that of his peers. Years later, when I taught his twin siblings, I asked them about him. At the time, Steven was twenty-five.

"Steven's doing ok." His brother Brad replied. "He took a few courses at Phoenix College, but dropped out."

"Where does he live?" I asked.

"With us. He sleeps out on the balcony."

"Does he wear a jacket?"

"Never Ms. P!"

Weeks later, when I drove by the Circle K, I saw Steven sitting outside on its concrete steps, with dirty blond dreadlocks, gulping what appeared to be a Slushy. His face was tilted toward the harsh Arizona sun. He was shirtless. I still hang onto the jacket.

Mary G. Powell lives in Phoenix, Arizona, and has been married to her high school sweetheart, Jerame Powell, for fourteen years. Mary has taught high school English for eleven years. She was a 2011 Frederick Douglass Scholar at West Chester University in Pennsylvania, where she taught a young adult literature course to pre-service English teachers. Mary has published an array of articles on her classroom within various publications including *English Journal* and *Teaching & Learning: The Journal of Natural Inquiry & Reflective Practice*. She is earning her Ph.D. in English education from Arizona State University. Mary is writing her dissertation on the impact of a writing community on teachers' identities as educators and as writers entitled, *The Right to Write: Novice English Teachers Write to Explore their Identities in a Writing Community*. She can be reached at *marygpowell@cox.net*.

What I Want to Believe

Todd Percinek

It was a dreary, bleak spring. The third day of stormy, lightening-filled skies. Rain was pounding the roof, and my students' identities were complex and nuanced. They entered the room, the second period of the day, in their sweats and with saturated hair, each commenting on the weather outside. Tanya stopped on the carpet before reaching her desk and shook her body furiously, like a drenched animal. Water flew everywhere. She did the same with her hair. Then she took off her pants—thankfully shorts were underneath—and shook them too, carelessly spraying two students near her although they didn't object. Then she draped her pants over the back of a chair near her seat.

I quickly assessed the situation, sensing a classroom atmosphere I recognized; if I tried to teach, it would not go well. I had learned much during two years of trying to determinedly plow through general English lessons no matter what the cost. This day needed to be a game day. As I pulled out *Apples to Apples*, *Boggle*, and *Scrabble*, my conscience was nagging at me. This is not rigorous. What would your colleagues think? You should be building writing skills. Here is a moment that exemplifies all that is wrong with public education. This is not an appropriate use of academic time.

General English is a class that shows up on the schedules of juniors and seniors unable to pass the district's writing graduation demonstration exam—the gatekeeper to a high school diploma. Seeing their peers enrolled in elective English courses of their own choosing, General English infuriates them because writing does not come easy and low self-concept runs deep. They already have attempted the exam at least four to six times. The course is notoriously known throughout the district as one of the most difficult English courses to teach. When teachers reference "Gen E," a common understanding reverberates. My department chair and I had a discussion about teachers' struggles with the course. We understood yet were frustrated by teachers who taught the course but refused the next year or gave up on students through a lack of rigor. We decided we would teach general English, each taking a section in order to learn about the course, the students, and find innovative ways to help them be successful. United, we moved forward. I stumbled over what I thought I knew and believed.

The students gathered in groups, choosing the game of their preference, needing no instruction from me. Today was automatic. Their conversations about life scattered around the room, oblivious to the passing period bell and the fact that I hadn't given any directions aside from saying good morning. I joined the group who liked to play "Speed Scrabble," and, as we set up the board, our conversation quickly turned to the use of behavior modification medication.

I learned that Drake refused to take his A.D.D. medication because he hated how it made him feel; he just wasn't himself. When he did take it, he complained he couldn't eat during the day and then would get crazy hunger binges late at night. No longer taking the pills, he claimed he had been conditioned to eat regularly late at night and gained a lot of weight as a result. Weeks earlier, I had called every student over to a corner of the room to conference with me about his or her progress in class while everyone else was writing. Out of the students in this class, he was one of three who had not yet passed the writing exam. But he was the most capable. Drake was demoralized.

"Drake, out of all the people in this class, I know you can do this," I said.

"I know."

"You're the most capable."

"I know I can pass the test."

I nodded.

"So what's up? What's going on?" I asked.

He slowly shook his head, eyes wandering, looking down. His round face and frazzled, short, blond hair with the cowlick in the back made him seem like a fifth grader rather than a junior in high school. He kicked his left foot forward, lightly tapping the leg of the table with the sole of his shoe.

He just couldn't motivate himself.

I expressed concern that I saw the same thing. "What about your other classes?" I asked. "Are you able to motivate yourself in your other classes?"

I already knew the answer. I needed to hear him answer.

"Same in my other classes," Drake said.

"I was wondering," I said. "Tell me more."

He couldn't understand what was happening to him.

"Drake, have you talked to your parents? Have you expressed these feelings to them? Have you told them what you just told me?"

He said he had. I inquired about their response.

"My parents didn't help me," he said.

After two terms, I finally saw an opening. I made my move.

"Would you feel comfortable talking to someone other than your parents?"

"Yes." Drake met me with direct, sustained eye contact. In that moment, I wanted to believe that he knew that I knew he was depressed. His eyes spoke relief. We discussed his comfort level with speaking to his counselor at school, and I told Drake I would contact her, letting her know that he would be stopping by. He didn't want to talk to her that day. I mentioned the resources his counselor could provide, saying talking to her was a positive starting place for trying to solve how he was feeling.

Now, in the middle of Speed Scrabble, Drake was open about his issue with eating, his storied past with Adderall, and how he felt about his body image. Tanya concurred with Drake's A.D.D. medication experiences. She had never been shy about her use of prescription drugs for focus. It was not uncommon for her to shout out in class—at the most inopportune times—to ask if she could leave to take her pills. Generally, she popped multiple pills at one time, announcing to the class and me how many she had taken to help her focus. Today, she agreed with Drake that pills made her different. She wasn't herself when she took them.

"You *know*, Mr. Pernicek. You've seen me." A slow, mischievous smile took over her pretty, carefully done-up face.

It was true. I had seen her, both when she had taken her medication and when she hadn't. When she hadn't taken her pills, Tanya was the student who never failed to shock me in class, doing the most outlandish things. One day, I looked up during small group work time, and she was hanging upside down in her chair. Her back was flat on the seat, legs against the chair back, and head dangling so she could look at the room upside down. I gave her my best teacher look—the Mr. Pernicek half-frown-question look, lips pressed together, tilted mouth, and wrinkled forehead. She had looked at me, head inverted, and broke into a small grin with a twinkle in her eye.

"Really?" I questioned. I shook my head back and forth for emphasis.

"What?" she said.

When Tanya took her medication, she was silent and docile. Focus was what drove her, and no one was able to interrupt. She didn't talk. Often she was silent an entire class period. And she could really produce writing. She definitely wasn't herself, but, at least, she wasn't hanging in a chair. I worried about her casual and incorrect use of prescription mediation. I had forwarded this concern to many in the bureaucracy meant to intervene in kids' lives. She was still popping pills.

"Yes," I said. "I've seen what you're like when you don't take your pills."

She continued to smile at me.

"I wonder what it would be like if you tried to focus without your pills. I get that it might be difficult, but, if you really wanted to focus on your own, do you think you could do it?"

"Maybe."

She expressed she didn't want Ritalin and was supposed to take it on a regular schedule but had already made up her mind not to. Her mom counted the pills in the bottle daily, for assurance that she was taking them. Tanya flushed pills so her mom thinks she was. And then, when she felt like she really couldn't focus, she would pop a few.

I finally saw an opening. I made my move.

"How many are you supposed to take?" I asked.

"Only one." She smiled again.

"I would be careful," I said. "Do you know how medication is supposed to work?"

Silence. The smile was still frozen.

I continued, explaining to Tanya and the other students around the Scrabble board how medication works. I told them you want a steady level built up in your system, and a level that is maintained so that it stays consistent. I added that is why you are supposed to take mediation in certain intervals, not skipping dosages or taking more than required in a certain amount of time. I said that when you don't maintain that consistency in your system and take medication sporadically, it could be ineffective, or even worse, cause more issues. I shared my opinion that you should either follow the directions for medication or not take it at all.

Tanya looked at me blankly. In that moment, I wanted to believe she heard me and understood.

"I agree," Drake said. "It can be dangerous."

Spencer jumped into the conversation. "I don't take my meds."

Spencer was like that. He was jittery. His eyes tended to wander all over the place like he was searching for something, not fully present in the moment but wanting to be. I wondered if he was searching for himself, somewhere, buried underneath a world of living. The trouble was that no one wanted to listen to Spencer. He was annoying. Other students couldn't stand him, and, every time there was group collaboration, he was left out. When there was a new seating chart, I could count on students approaching me, expressing the dire importance they be moved because they couldn't sit next to him. They hated him. As a result, Spencer often chose to work by himself.

He comfortably attempted the work I asked him to do, alone. Slightly overweight, but not fat, with his perfectly cropped haircut, he sat in his chair silently, the model student. When he got stuck, he summoned me over to him by shouting across the room. Often, he only wanted reassurance he was on the right track. He always was.

This was an improvement because at the beginning of the term, he would just sit, eyes shifting. He refused to do any work at all. He wouldn't participate. He wouldn't write. He would repeatedly say he couldn't do things: "I can't hold a pencil," "My back hurts so I can't get my binder," or "I can't read because I'm tired." Constantly, he did his best to annoy teachers. He told me his goal was to get under their skin until they were irritated enough to kick him out of class.

He was effective at pushing others away, so he could be isolated. I had seen kids like him before in general English. I knew the drill. I knew all the tricks of the trade. I portrayed calm on the outside while my mind was screaming in hopes of shaking rationality into him. Yet, there were times—some of my worst times as a teacher—when he baited me and I went for it. I lashed out words: "Spencer, shut your mouth! You're not cool!" or "Since you can't take a hint and obviously don't understand my subtlety, let me spell it out for you: you're being a pain, so do us all a favor and just stop!" He retreated in those moments, signaling I had lost what I believe. I always apologized later, sharing with him my deep regret for how I acted while still acknowledging my undeniable feelings.

I knew, more than anything, he needed me to relate to him, take note of him, and let him know it was O.K. to be him. Yet it was infuriating to listen to his incessant bad-boy posturing, interrupting every lesson or discussion to proclaim how high he once got or how angry he was when he punched a wall or how he got pulled over by the cops. When he shared these moments he lit up, eyes springing to life, a gigantic grin encompassing his face. Every teacher and student in the building believed Spencer made everything up. I was unsure if these proclamations were real or invented. In reality, there was some truth to his situation. He needed the people he was pushing away.

That rainy day, after we put the board games away, we transitioned to the computer lab for the second half of class to continue writing from the previous day. Spencer was staring at a blank screen. Actually, Spencer did this more than he wrote. But so did many of the General English students. I went over to him and knelt down next to him.

"Hey, guy, how can I help you?" I asked.

"I don't know what to write. I can't write today."

"O.K." It was one of those days. I had no idea what my entry point was to get Spencer to talk. Why wasn't he motivated? I used to think kids like Spencer were defiant, resisting me, my class, my teaching. I knew better now. This was much deeper than defiance. "Tell me what I *can* do?"

Pause. I waited. There were so many other students I could have been helping.

"Nothing."

"O.K. You let me know when you are ready," I said. I walked away, knowing I would momentarily be back kneeling next to him. I made my rounds. Spencer was still staring at his blank screen. I approached again, asking how things were going for him.

"Mr. P., I'm not going to write today."

"Why not?"

He revealed that he was in legal trouble. Again. This time, he was contemplating agreeing to a sentence of seven days in jail because, according to him, then the situation would be over, and he could purge it from his mind. I asked when he went before the judge with his plea, and Spencer told me it was later that day. I learned the most recent event leading to his current troubles unfolded at a gas station. Somehow, a physical altercation had erupted between Spencer and another man in a convenience store, and the employee had asked them to get out. They had continued fighting in the parking lot, and the cops were called. Spencer was ticketed for assault.

The assignment was to write a narrative, recreating the action for the reader. I suggested Spencer write a narrative about the fight and the police showing up.

"I'll write tomorrow, Mr. P. I just can't get things out of my mind today."

That entire conversation took place without our eyes ever meeting. We existed in the same space, but he, again, wasn't fully present.

I looked up, and Casey walked into the computer lab. It appeared as if he had just arrived at school; he still had a backpack and a coat on. The storm got him, too; water was dripping from every part of his thin frame. His usually frizzy, shoulder-length brown curls were still there amidst the weight of dampness. His pimpled face expressionless, he slowly, without saying anything to anyone, walked across the computer lab and made his way to a computer. Most of the students paid him no attention. A few said "hi" and returned to what they were doing.

I needed to approach him delicately. Situations like this could be explosive, causing general English students to scream, throw things, or storm out of the room yelling "fuck you" before slamming the door. I used to immediately have late students sign their tardy card, stressing to them the importance of getting to class on time, keeping everything strictly business. I knew better now.

"Good morning Casey. I'm happy you're here today. It's good to see you."

He humphed. Then he quickly glanced at me, looking away. This could have ended up going two ways: extremely well, with our relationship intact or his shutting me out for good. I wasn't in control. This was up to him.

"What happened this morning? Is everything OK?"

"Mr. P, it's a really bad day."

"I'm sorry, man. That stinks. It's never good when you have to start your day in a bad way. I hate bad mornings. They are the worst because, for me, they ruin my entire day."

Silence. I waited.

More silence. I tried again.

"Why was it a bad morning?" I asked.

Casey finally started talking. He said his parents had come home drunk, again. This time it was two in the morning, and they had woken him up. They fought all night long, yelling at each other, again, like they do when they are drunk. He couldn't fall asleep until 4:30 in the morning, and then he didn't hear his alarm. He had just woken up about an hour ago. I empathized, reiterating I was pleased he made it to school because some students dealing with a similar situation the night before would have just stayed home. I filled him in on the assignment, and he said he was not sure if he was going to be able to write today.

"For obvious reasons," he said with a shrug, a simple gesture communicating more than I can understand. I nodded. A straightforward indication of assurance was all I could give in return.

Decency was what Casey needed that eerie stormy day, and my conversation with him was time well spent, for both of us. These students are snapshots of larger populations wounded by life and school. They don't need control. They need trust. A class like general English is a scab amidst too many life wounds, a constant marker, reminding students they are bad at writing.

With their trust, we can move forward together.

Todd Pernicek received a B.S. in secondary education and an M.A. from the University of Nebraska-Lincoln. He has taught high school English and reading classes for seven years. During his brief time in the classroom, he has been inspired and challenged by his students to regularly reconsider what it means to be an effective literacy teacher. He is currently on leave from the Lincoln Public Schools in Lincoln, Nebraska, where he resides with his wife.

The Year of My Fourth Dimension

Kathy Yocum

I love teaching science. That is a deep, honest statement, but the written words don't convey how I feel. Written in all caps, I LOVE TEACHING SCIENCE, is a shout-out to the world as pure joyful truth. My goal in teaching is to do my best to help students leave me with, at minimum, an "a-ha" spark of interest in science. At best, they develop a thriving curiosity and an insatiable appetite. The reality is that a few students leave my class with little more than relief at having gotten one step closer to graduation. I can't win them all, but the teacher in me *always* keeps trying.

My eighth year of teaching delivered to my classroom two students who surpassed my expectations for student's love of science.

They arrived as an odd pair. The first, I'll call Sam, was a thin, five foot three, stringy haired blond, teeth adorned by braces, with a thin barely-there little scruff of chin hair meant to serve as a young man's first attempt as a beard. The second, I'll call Charlie, was almost opposite of Sam. He had a beautiful head full of red hair, a little on the heavy side, glasses slipping down the bridge of his nose, and a constant smile. His six feet towered over his best friend and me, his teacher. I knew them both since I had taught them chemistry. They had been good students, but neither showed much of the spark I so desperately want to see on the faces of my students. Sam and Charlie were not your typical isolated nerds, but they were nerds. They were likeable guys. They mixed well in the student population, and both of them walked girlfriends up and down the hallways of our school.

Here Sam and Charlie were today, supplies in hand, and ready to get started in physics. This was my second year to teach the subject. I was qualified to teach it, but it takes more than one year for me to get in a confident rhythm with class enrichment activities to reach the students and get them to the "a-ha" moment. I was still working to refine the course. Along with sixteen other students, they were ready for class to begin. I look out at the classroom thinking, "This is good.

There are more students taking physics than last year. That's a positive sign."

To my relief, the first few weeks rolled smoothly by. Most of this time is a refresher of foundational science and developing the math skills we would be using. I've learned that, in physics, this is the point where students may choose to drop the subject. For the most part, it's the math that scares them. I repeat religiously, "Math and science are married. Math proves the science as truth." There sit the pair; math is no problem for them. They wanted more. Oh, my heart swelled. Are these the "insatiables" I have dreamed of? Nope, they were more.

I know I am supposed to be careful in what I ask for because I just may get it. With this pair, I got it. What a joy. They were more than I had dreamed of but also my biggest challenge. It wasn't a matter of student behavior; it was a challenge for me to keep up with these two. Oh, it started innocently enough with vectors. If you are not familiar with vectors, it is basically showing direction and magnitude of motion using lines and arrows to illustrate. It helps the written problems make visual sense. To help me, I had taken the problems, worked them out in the weeks or nights ahead of teaching, and appeared in class with completed work in neat plastic sleeves. I was prepared for all of my students *except* for these two. If the work gave the slightest room for a different interpretation, these two saw it, reworked it, illustrated it, and frequently confused the remainder of the class. One half of me cheered them on with, "Keep going! Keep going!" while the other half was moaning "Oh, boys, don't complicate this for the others." We worked out a compromise where they would not rework the white board, but I would be sure I had time to see where their fascinating brains had taken them.

Teaching physics was no longer my only job. I had to become a voracious reader of science material. I couldn't read deeply; I had to read broadly and quickly. Before school began, I, thankfully, finished Joy Hakim's *The Story of Science: Newton at the Center*. Her work is a great read with short science vignettes carrying us through science discoveries over time and loaded with lots of interesting asides. Once I began working with Sam and Charlie, I immediately ordered the other two books in her series. My home was *my* homework center. In the evenings, I'd scan several science websites. Stephen Hawking sometimes joined Hakim's work and Bill Bryson's, *A Short History of Nearly Everything*. Theirs were words that took me to dreamland. I didn't have to know everything, but these boys wanted to talk about a variety of science topics. They were amazing.

Lunchtime that year was nonexistent. Here stood Sam and Charlie at my white board with my precious white board markers going on about their chosen topic of the day. But their obsessively favorite topic was the fourth dimension. All those hours of reading and reviewing, and I never got it. I couldn't even disguise the confused expression on my face. It still makes no sense. Here are these great thinkers trying to sketch on a two-dimensional board a four dimensional concept. Shading and construing a graphic can give the illusion of a three dimensional object. But four dimensions? By the way, the girlfriends were smart enough to avoid these sessions.

Project labs were great. Grouping was never a problem. I'd give the topic and guidelines and off the two of them went. They didn't always work alone. If students expressed curiosity in what they were thinking, these two embraced them. The pair became a threesome or foursome, and great learning took place for us all.

Cleaning up after labs, however, became a problem. For projectile motion, we created trebuchets from materials I supplied. The boys wanted bigger and better. I gave them a second kit, telling them, "Here is what I can supply. Go for your own design." The marshmallow toss activity was performed as I had planned with class members cheering on their design, measuring and calculating carefully. Then the big guns were brought out. Sam and Charlie presented a huge, clunky, but impressively accurate, trebuchet. Their work station was cluttered and piled with wood and bungee scraps, nails, screws, electric tools, and who knew what else. It was filled with so much stuff, I retrieved the largest janitorial trash can I could find and dictated, "OK guys, this is your mess to clear." Near the end of the electric house project, they had brought and dismantled two appliances for the motors, incorporated a turntable from an old record player, and had wire scraps and diodes scattered far and wide. By this time, our kind janitor had supplied me with a broom and dustpan and checked with me weekly about clean up days.

My years of teaching since have not produced anyone quite like Sam and Charlie. Maybe I just received my wish of a lifetime midway through my teaching career. I readily admit that the boys gave me credit for being more knowledgeable than I am. I was just limping along trying to keep up. My heart knew they were seeking someone to listen, someone that appreciated their passion and loved the subject. I am so deeply grateful to them for letting me be that someone.

They went on to college and would occasionally call me just to chat. I knew they were in good hands and had found others to keep the spark of their passion burning. By now, they have entered careers of their choosing. And, because they weren't the typical nerds, I hope they now have families of their own. My wish for them is for each to produce a mini copy of themselves. I want to believe there is a new generation of fourth dimension obsessives out there. Maybe they can one day explain it, so I can understand

Kathy Yocum teaches at Natchitoches Central High School in Natchitoches, Louisiana. She earned her bachelor's degree from Mississippi University for Women and a master of science degree from Louisiana Tech. Kathy serves on her school improvement team and on the District S.T.E.M. committee for grant writing through the Orchard Foundation. She recently became a teacher consultant with the Northwestern State University Writing Project Summer Institute. Kathy is in her fifteenth year of teaching. She began teaching family and consumer science but soon found what she calls her "true love"— science. After going back to college, she has earned teaching certification in chemistry, physics and, most recently, advanced placement chemistry. Kathy's other passions are her three granddaughters who she refers to as "my three little women." She along with her cat, Newton, enjoy evenings on her deck on the banks of Cane River Lake in Natchitoches, Louisiana.

Althrea Tells Me Gangs Mean Love

Mark Gozonsky

The assignment for today's class is to teach me something I don't already know. Althrea tells me gangs mean love. Love as in caring, love as in listening, love as in love songs. Other people have told me gangs mean love before, but I just couldn't process the words. It was like they were telling me sand is cheese, or music is a mustache. But I believe Althrea because she told me to read *The Coldest Winter Ever,* and I trust people when they tell you a book is good, and it actually turns out to be good. Althrea—who looks like she could have been telling stories in Kenyan moonlight a thousand years ago—doesn't mean gangs mean all love all the time. But neither do the kindest moms or best role-model dads or even the cutest little babies. Everybody knows all the bad things about gangs, but, if you think about the love part, then you have to think of what else gangs might mean besides what you already know. Here's what I've been thinking.

***

I'm charmed one day to see M'decio wearing a University of Texas sweatshirt. My daughter has worn her own U.T. sweatshirt to her school that very day, and the matching sweatshirts symbolize cross-cultural equity in a way that feels like eating delicious homemade soup. The next day I notice a few more kids at our school wearing U.T. sweatshirts, and soon it's like when you buy a new car and start seeing your model everywhere. So, I type in "University of Texas sweatshirt gangs" and sure enough…

I am very disappointed to discover that M'Decio is probably not an aspiring Longhorn, although he could be. While we were watching the movie *Which Way Home,* he wrote an empathetic essay about Latin American children migrating to the U.S. riding on top of trains. No one should have to live that way, he wrote. It makes you appreciate the things we have. It makes you want to do something, if only you knew what could be done.

I wrote M'Decio a Post-it note in praise of his insight and structure. This was not the first such Post-it I had written to him, but they were not enough to prevent his rampant absences, and I worried about what he was doing while he was away.

***

Another thing I have been thinking about, since believing Althrea that gangs mean love, is that conflict in the world comes from trying to separate good from evil, evil from good. I didn't make this up myself; I read it somewhere this year, but, now, I can't remember where. I did, however, just recently come across a note I wrote to the counselor of another student, Simon.

"He does nothing in class but write gang insignia and brag about his gang activities."

It was incongruous coming from Simon due to his baby face and braces, but there he was, always whispering to classmates about people he'd seen getting shot. Althrea used to mock him for being a fake gangster, but that didn't stop him from spending the first ten and last ten minutes of each class period, and most of the time in between, trying to convince us all he was the real thing.

The thing about Simon was his docility. He had the quiet of rot from within. First semester, he sat next to his nice-girl girlfriend and did no work. He did *epic* no work. Class after class, doing nothing except desultorily taking up my interventions just long enough for me to get involved with another student. Then he went back to doing nothing. Teaching him was like turning on a water sprinkler in the Mojave.

What finally worked with Simon was teaming up with his counselor, Mrs. Wilson. I was so surprised when Mrs. Wilson won a student award for "Most Likely to Smile to Hide Her True Feelings." I always figured she was happy. Mrs. Wilson told me she was happy I brought the problem with Simon to her attention. Talking to her just cheered me up so much that I sat down with Simon and wrote essays with him line-by-line. I wrote a line on my paper; he wrote a line on his.

Simon said, "The guy in this story is really street smart, Mister, but the school doesn't care about what he knows. Who does that remind you of?"

I gazed upon his chubby cheeks. "No one?"

"Think harder," he told me. I promised to try. I introduced the "Simon A" to class, which meant any time he turned in work of C quality or higher, everyone else in class got an extra credit A. He turned out to have a talent for expressing his perspective, which was rebellion and dog-eat-dog oriented. Mrs. Wilson had told me he dreamed of becoming a firefighter. When I was out of other ideas, I told him, "Pass the class, Simon, so you can follow your dream to become a firefighter."

He said, "I know you're talking to Mrs. Wilson because she tells me that too."

"Yeah, we're ganging up on you," I told him. He wound up passing the class. We nodded or waved to each other in the hall, both smiling.

***

Tyrane did *nothing* on the final. He had been pointed out to me as a gang member by the brilliantly smiling center fielder on the first day I went to baseball practice. In fact, brilliantly smiling Donovan pointed to just about every other kid on the field and told me of their gang affiliations. I was happy when Donavan turned up in my second semester class, but he then proceeded to skip so often that I had to call his mom once a week to get him to class often enough to pass, which he did by doing classwork quite proficiently the final month and also doing well on the final.

Tyrane, in contrast, did nothing on the final, which was what he had done in class all year, except for the time when I had them build arguments out of craft sticks. He had said he was good at building stuff, why couldn't I have them build stuff instead of writing. He built a solid structure involving *pathos*, *logos* and *ethos*. I sent a picture of him giving a big thumbs up to my dad. ("White guys love giving a big thumbs up," I heard him explain later.) But, since I had sent that photo to my father, I felt I couldn't give up on or decide to hate Tyrane, even though he was always disruptive in class, feeling up the girls and complaining that I wasn't teaching shit.

Even when he failed too many courses to stay eligible for the baseball team. Still, he had thrown strikes during one batting practice, he had hit some line drives. I had been there for that; I had witnessed that. I couldn't ignore the facts of his proficiency in baseball despite his flagrant hatred for classroom participation. So, after he turns in nothing on the final, despite my Post-its urging him "Try this part—it's easy and you can do enough to pass"—I rearrange it so he can read an excerpt from *Black Boy* out loud and identify its elements of immediacy, such as setting, dialogue, emotion, physical sensation and so on. At first he says, "I'm not gonna be able to do this," but I convince him to start reading, and we take it from there.

***

Let me finish by talking about M'decio again. I don't think I mentioned him dancing in my black cowboy hat on the last day of school before winter vacation. He did, and I took this as such a good sign of a lowered affective filter. But, then, in second semester, he was so hit or miss with attendance, I really became very skeptical about him. I questioned his purpose and integrity. I thought he was probably involved with gangs.

But he was on the J.V. team, and I kept a special reserve of caring for baseball players. I had to do this in order to justify my being there, because otherwise, if being the assistant coach didn't result in extra caring, then what the hell was I doing there? The whole point of my standing out there on that weedy baseball field for hours every afternoon was to demonstrate caring for those boys. And not just demonstrate it but to actually care. I felt that every hour we spent taking batting practice was an hour they spent not pursuing gang-related activities. This was the most explicit awareness I had all year of gang activity at my school this year—that the guys on the baseball team were being diverted from it by playing ball.

One day M'decio and I played catch. Did I tell you I had incredible difficulty in throwing the ball straight sometimes? M'decio was standing next to a chain link fence, and I kept throwing the ball on the other side of the fence. My mechanics were off, and so were his: he kept lofting the ball way over my head. I hustled after it. Much of my coaching technique this year consisted of demonstrating hustle.

M'decio was an especially grim fellow to watch strike out. He would take this odd, stiff-elbowed lunge, miss the ball by a yard, then have this glassy-looking laughter expression, like every time he failed it was funny.

On the last day of school, we go on a field trip to see the Dodgers, who had invited us to watch them taking batting practice. They keep us behind a rope which kind of sucks, but the geometry of the experience, being on the same plane as home plate, is still exultant. M'decio sits behind me during the game which is good because none of the other baseball players are sitting anywhere near me. We discuss the stupendous base-running errors perpetrated willy-nilly by both the home team and the visiting Angels. Game over, we head back to school and wait for parents to pick the kids up. This happens g-r-a-d-u-a-l-l-y. M'decio says he can walk home, although this will certainly mean getting robbed of the stray ball he nabbed during batting practice.

"And your clothes," says Sam.

"And all your money," says Eugene.

"They might take you and just leave your clothes," says Hiram. M'decio laughs at the image of a pile of clothes where he used to be.

"I can give you a lift," I say, and, once all the other kids are picked up, I do. The streets are empty. We see one guy jog by, and we're glad we're not him. It's quiet, the trees are tall, the streets are black, and the silence seems very interruptible.

"You can just drop me here at the liquor store; it's just a block from home," M'decio says. That's fine. What kid ever wants to be dropped off exactly where he's going?

"Have a good summer," I tell him.

"Be safe," he tells me.

Mark Gozonsky earned a B.A. in English at Cornell and took a class in journalism at San Francisco State before getting a part-time job covering the A's and Giants with Jimmy Ilson for *Calendar*, the forerunner to *SF Weekly*. After moving to Texas, he became editor of *Practical Supervision* and, after moving to Los Angeles, a commentator on public radio's *Marketplace*. He was editor of *America Online's Digital City LA* during the late 1990s, until his twin daughters entered kindergarten and summoned him to become a teacher. He's been with the Los Angeles Unified School District since 2002. Mark has published fiction recently in *Switchback*, *Two Hawks Quarterly*, *Corium*, and *The Furnace Review*. His essay, "Althrea Tells Me Gangs Mean Love," which was originally published by *Indiana English*, was written during the summer of 2011, while Mark worked as a fellow in the U.C.L.A. Writing Project.

Teaching Means Seeing In Different Ways

Teaching Spanish and Learning Latino

Amanda Marek

"In the story from the previous question, is the protagonist more like the tortoise or the hare?"

    a. the hare, because she is overconfident
    b. the tortoise, because she's persistent
    c. the tortoise, because she's too slow to win
    d. the hare, because she's the fastest"

I look over my student's shoulder as she scrolls her cursor over each answer—abcd, abcd, abcd. She finally clicks 'c' and moves on to the next question, annoyed and confused because she knows the slow protagonist did win the race but can't make sense of the other answers. I sigh, knowing she's never heard of the tortoise, the hare, or any of Aesop's fables. She's lived in Minnesota all her life, but her parents don't speak English. The stories she grew up with are "La llorona" and "Los tres consejos." I look around the computer lab full of Hispanic[1] students and wonder how many of their answers are indicating that they can't read when their real obstacle is that they don't have a white middle class background. It counts against them on standardized tests, in their classes, in the hallways, and at the park; a constant series of "ticks" pointing out that they don't measure up to what Minnesota expects of them. The next day, I will comfort this student, whose reading score will have dropped fifteen points because she doesn't know that the tortoise won the race through persistence. Ironic, considering she's still persistently trying to pull respectable grades in a community that doesn't believe she's capable of academic success.

I am not an ELL teacher. I do not teach in an urban school. My school is a grades eight and nine junior high in a relatively small, but rapidly growing, third-ring suburb. It has a quaint main street, a tight community of families who have lived there for generations, and a relatively large immigrant population of Russians and Hispanics. I used to teach ninth grade English and Spanish I. This year I started teaching ninth grade English and Spanish for Native Speakers (SNS). My SNS class is blocked with English, so I have these kids for two hours—one hour of English 9 and one of Spanish. And I'm the blond *gringa* who's going to teach them Spanish.

At the beginning of the year, that's definitely how they saw me. I was the only white person in the room. Class felt like something out of *Dangerous Minds* or *Freedom Writers*. I'd try to get their attention to start class, and they'd glance at me before continuing their conversations unperturbed, scattered in clusters around the room based on gang affiliation or avoidance thereof. But two hours a day in one class with a teacher who had the patience and persistence of Aesop's tortoise caught their attention, and, before long, they realized I wasn't giving up. Better yet, I understood where they were coming from or at least I wanted to. I think the kicker was when I went to Nicaragua over fall break with a Rotary Club delegation and came back with pictures and stories and tears in my eyes. They saw the value I placed in the Spanish language and in a Hispanic culture. Soon enough, I was the teacher they came to for everything.

"Ms. Marek, I need a tampon."

"Ms. Marek, can I come in after school and talk to you about some things?"

"Ms. Marek, a boy just chased me down the hallway and told me to go back to Mexico."

"Ms. Marek, what do you do if your boyfriend hits you? It's not me…it's a friend."

And so, for two hours a day, we were our own little micro-community. It was fascinating for me to have a class entirely of Hispanic students. One day early in the year, I looked around my classroom, chewing my lip, as I took in the completely dysfunctional literature circles. Graciela and Elisa had turned their chairs, so they didn't have to face each other. Luz and Ana sat side by side on the floor, reading from the same book. Marco and Guillermo glared at each other across the room, ignoring their respective groups. Lit circles were not going to work if this kept up, and, for some reason, simply telling them that they had to learn to work with people they didn't get along with didn't have the impact it did in the rest of my classes. I had to figure out what was going on. I knelt down next to Selena. "What's going on here?" I interrupted her reading and motioned to the groups around us. She blinked once, looked at me and then around the room.

"Is working in groups that terrible?"

"You gotta know your groups, Ms. Marek."

"What do you mean?"

"Well…" She glanced around the room looking for an example. "Elisa's cousin jumped Graciela's brother last year, and Graciela's parents sent him back to Mexico. They're not gonna work together."

"Hm." I nodded. "What's going on here?" I pointed to Luz and Ana.

"Ana shared her locker with Amelia, but then they got in a fight, and Amelia took all her books."

I frowned, wondering what other classes of Luz's were being affected by this. "And Marco and Guillermo?" Selena looked at me, hesitating. "They're not even in a group together. What's going on there?"

"Can't talk about that." Selena tried to go back to her book.

"Why not?"

"I don't wanna get them in trouble."

I sighed. "Selena, I need to know what's going on. I won't let them know you told me anything, and, unless they are currently planning to hurt each other, I won't get them in trouble." I really hoped she wasn't going to tell me anything I would have to report. "If I'm going to teach this class, I need to know what's causing all of this." Selena held my gaze, a defiant look on her face, debating whether she could trust me.

"Marco's a Sureño and Guillermo's a King," she said finally.

"Oh." I knew what this meant. Los Sureños 13 and Los Reyes Latinos (Latin Kings or LKs) are rival Latino gangs in our community. Generally, the LKs had numbers that kept the Sureños from challenging them, but the Sureños had been increasing their own numbers this year. I also already knew that Marco indicated Sureño; the signs were all over his notebooks.

"Selena, I need to know who all is gang-affiliated. I won't say anything, but I need to know where the lines are drawn so that I can make this classroom a safe place and keep the focus on learning." Selena studied me again, but didn't deliberate quite so long this time.

"Okay. I'll come in after school." Selena did indeed come in, and she told me what she knew regarding who was in a gang, who wanted to be, who avoided gangs, and even some of the family affiliations of the girls who took care to stay away from gang activity. She didn't know everyone's story, but it was enough so that between gang signs engraved on my desks, seating charts, and what she told me, I had a pretty good idea of what I would see in my room for the rest of the year. Armed with this information, I was able to put together more cohesive groups for the next round of lit circles. I incorporated different types of small group work and team building throughout the year; by the end, the kids often—though not always—left gang conflicts at the door. I also knew that I would need to find ways to integrate education about gangs into the curriculum. *Romeo and Juliet* lent itself quite well to that, and, since the ninth grade English team was using it to address how classical literature influences contemporary literature, *West Side Story* was even better. The kids could really relate to the movie at the level of gang rivalry, they understood the jokes and the stereotypes within Latino culture that went over the heads of the rest of my classes, and they were moved by Maria's monologue at the end.

By working with them, asking questions, and earning their trust and therefore honesty, I learned so much about how their cultures functioned as a subculture in Minnesota. I saw how they had adapted their Mexican, Guatemalan, and Salvadorian cultures to a general Latino culture, and how they further adapted it to mesh with what Minnesota demanded of them. And I, too, became part of this culturally mish-mashed community.

In other ways, I was already the expert. Culturally, I had the academic knowledge that Columbus's discovery of the New World and its riches had precipitated an onslaught of European invasion, half of which was determined to strip the Americas of all they had to offer, and the other half of which went forth to educate the "heathens" and make them civilized and Christian. I had a very wide, if shallow, knowledge of Latin American holidays and customs and how each stemmed from its own unique mix of European and indigenous cultures. The kids didn't know all this, even though they are the living consequences of it.

So I tried to teach them the history of their various cultures while they taught me the present of them. During the day, I had them use graphic organizers to help them see the European and indigenous influences on the Mexican holiday *día de los reyes magos,* or Three Kings Day, and how the holiday reflects cultural perspectives. After school, Elisa, Ana and Ernesto made a career of trying to teach me to dance *bachata* and *cumbia.* Ana would slowly walk me through the steps, while Elisa and Ernesto danced together to show me how it looked faster and with a partner.

"Uno – dos – tres – cuatro – cinco – seis – siete – ocho – uno – dos – tres – muy bien, maestra, you got it!" Ana was encouraging. Elisa was more critical.

"Ms. Marek, you gotta move your *hips!*"

"I thought I was…" I would reply. Then in my attempt to move my hips, I would lose the steps.

No matter how many times they showed me, I still couldn't dance without embarrassing myself at their quinceañeras.

Linguistically, I was the expert because I had studied Spanish; I knew the patterns, the etymology, and the grammar, where they only knew what sounded "right" based on whatever they'd heard growing up. Veronica, in particular, constantly tried to correct my Spanish. Sometimes she was right, especially when my pronunciation suffered as a result of trying to read aloud and manage the classroom at the same time. "Ms. Marek, es simpatic*ooo,* no simpatic*aaa!*" But when it came to grammar, she was often incorrect. "Ms. Marek, es sabe, no sepa!"

"Thank you, Veronica, but it is actually 'sepa' because I need the subjunctive form of the verb for this sentence."

Veronica would listen to my explanation with a quizzical look on her face. "But it sounds wrong." At this point in our conversation, I would have the difficulty of explaining that it sounded wrong because what she was hearing at home was incorrect grammar. How does one do that without appearing to question the intelligence or linguistic capabilities of a student's parent?

Other times, students made errors based on their own assumptions and inaccurate analyses of the languages, as when Luz told me that *te* means "it." Considering *te* is the direct pronoun form of "you," I asked her to use it in a sentence for me.

"I would say this to my brother," she started. "Te voy a quitar el juguete. I'm going to take *it*, the toy, from you."

"So where is 'you' in your sentence?" I asked, looking at her thoughtfully. Luz tilted her head to the right and stared off to the left, like she does when she's thinking hard.

"Te means you? I thought tú means you?" With a little further analysis, Luz figured out the correct meaning of *te* and also understood why she'd misinterpreted it.

But, despite my academic knowledge of linguistics, I was the only non-native speaker in the room. So, as I taught them grammar, reading, writing and spelling in the language they had acquired in kitchens and at quinceañeras, they poked fun at my accent and taught me vocabulary, colloquialisms and folk stories that I could only have learned by living in each of their native countries. Our little community quickly turned into one of mutual benefit, as I learned just as much from them as they did from me.

I got to see these kids in ways other teachers didn't. I had them in a setting where they were comfortable. They all knew each other, even if they had their feuds, fallings out, and even gang rivalries. In my classroom, no one told them to go back to Mexico, no one made fun of the grammar mistakes they made in English or their accents, and no one assumed they were stupid because they didn't know an English word. They were safe. As a result, they were loud. They took risks, yelled out answers—sometimes while I was mid-sentence—and asked questions. They constantly asked for help in class, and I often had half of them in my classroom after school. I was surprised to hear from a paraprofessional sometime during third quarter how quiet they were in other classes and that they always kept under the radar. I wondered how other teachers saw these kids who I knew as precocious, confident, social and, often, melodramatic. I wonder, still, if they see the incredible potential in these kids, or if they just see the quiet kids who won't ask questions, who struggle to understand vocabulary, who only seem to come out of their shells in the hallway. I wondered what my colleagues thought about their parents who seldom show up for conferences—which says more about our supply of translators than their interest in their children's education. While I know my colleagues and I know them to be conscientious and compassionate, I do know the assumptions and stereotypes that are out there in the greater community. I also know the frustration of working with a student who struggles with some aspect of the subject and trying to find a better way to explain it. I've also experienced how easily students see and misread that frustration. And most importantly, I now know how these kids have picked up, and over the years internalized, assumptions about themselves and their ability to learn.

I would love to tell you that at the end of the year we all got along, regardless of gang affiliation, that the kids were seamlessly accepted into the greater junior high community, that they all earned straight A's and that their test scores were off the charts. But this isn't *Dangerous Minds* or *Freedom Writers*. This is one little class in a little third-ring suburb in Minnesota. What I can tell you is that my kids knew all year that for two hours a day, they were in a safe place. They knew they had an adult in their school to whom they could come with anything. They performed extremely well on standardized writing tests, and in most cases, their reading scores improved somewhere between noticeably and dramatically. But what was most gratifying for me this year is that they grew in self-knowledge and in confidence; they shared their dreams with me and started to hope that they could achieve them. Through their growth over the course of the year, they taught me that one tortoise-like teacher can help a diverse group of students turn stereotypes and conflicts into opportunities for rich discussion and obstacles into challenges that will ultimately teach them life's most important lessons.

Amanda Marek teaches ninth grade English and Spanish for native speakers in Shakopee, Minnesota. She received her B.A. in English and Spanish at the College of St. Benedict, participated in the Minnesota Writing Project, and is now working towards her M.A. in English at the University of St. Thomas. She has taught both English/language arts and Spanish as a foreign language at the middle and high school levels. After having traveled extensively in Spain, Nicaragua, Ecuador and Mexico, she has become interested in cultural and linguistic interdependence. In her teaching, she is particularly concerned with bilingual and bicultural literacy and education and works to give voice to her students' individual and cultural identities.

No Detectable Difference

Heather Adkins

Each year after standardized test scores are tallied, long after the students have left my classroom, and I no longer have any way of doing anything about what they did or did not learn, I have a little sit down with my principal to sign off on my value-added scores. I'm sure every state has a report similar to this, one that measures how much a teacher affected individual students based on a projection of how said students should have scored on the test based on how they scored years earlier. Ideally, three letters will follow the score: N.D.D. No Detectable Difference.

Often, it feels as though that this is what society and the government and whoever else chimes in on these discussions expects of teachers: that we approach education like quality control at a factory where not being able to tell who produced which product is a sign of success.

To someone like me, who pursued a career in teaching generally and teaching high school specifically so I could impact students' lives the way Mr. Callis and Ms. Clark did mine, the thought of sailing through on N.D.D.s saddens me.

These were my thoughts as I packed up my room at the end of the school year. My favorite student, one who had overcome so much—a bad home life, bad friends and a year spent in a juvenile detention center—and blossomed into a person who truly saw himself as a reader and a writer, had been arrested the night before. This time it was for allegedly raping a twelve-year-old girl. I had been so excited to see what he did next in life, to have him return to my classes and share his successes with other students. "From jail cells to awards, Mrs. A. Who'd a thought it?" He'd always say whenever he showed me a certificate he had earned for being the Star Student of the week or making the honor roll. And though the accomplishments were his, they made me feel successful, too. He was proof that my teaching methods worked. Looking at his empty chair on graduation night, I felt the acronym in the pit of my stomach. NDD. This student had both entered and exited the building with crime hanging over his head. And, despite my best efforts, my felt success, on paper he had not changed much. What a lovely way to end the school year.

But as I cleaned out my email, I saw a message from Shanesse, a student I taught for both junior and senior English. The email was more than six months old, and I was really surprised to see it had survived my sometimes brutal use of the delete key.

> *Hey it's Shanesse! How are you? And Avery and Kyle, and the house? I hope things are not too stressful for you! Well, I was writing another paper for my English class, and it made me think of your classes in high school. When I wrote my first paper for your class, it was terrible. The one on Puritan Society? I looked back at it a couple of weeks ago and it was seriously awful. I just didn't know how to write a paper. But, being in your class I feel like I learned how to write excellent papers, and I just wanted to say thanks! My English professor asked me what processes I went through to develop my papers as well as I have, and the only thing I could really tell him was that my English teacher in high school taught me how to write like that. And, I think your classes also helped me develop a love for writing, as well for English in general. I've changed my major to English, actually. I've decided to become an English teacher. I guess I just wanted to say thanks to one of my favorite teachers for being such a good teacher. I certainly wouldn't love English as much as I do if it weren't for you, and I owe a lot of my writing skill to you, as well. So, thanks again! I hope to hear from you soon!*
>
> *Sincerely,*
> *Shanesse*

Fat tears rolled down my cheeks unchecked. Here was a student saying I had affected the trajectory of her life. That she loved English, at least in part, because of me. That was why I had entered the classroom: to help kids learn to love learning.

Just below Shanesse's message was an email from Emily requesting I respond to a survey for an education class she was taking. At the end she added this:

P.S. I am loving school and I am in a British Literature class and my teacher is shocked that I have been introduced to so many works and I credit that to you. I also wanted to let you know that the way you tested us in AP English, having to figure out what work the passage came from and what the details were behind the passage, has really helped me in his class because that is the way he gives his exams! So thanks for preparing me for this! Hope this year is going well.

I signed off and powered down the computer. While I waited for it to finish so I could store the machine for the summer, my eye caught the little yellow sticky note taped to the bottom of my monitor:

I love you Mrs. Adkins!

Love, Liz.

I smiled. I'd recently received another note from Liz, this one a wedding invitation. Next on my list was my desk, a place notorious for being clean only on the first and last day of school. I dug through the drawers, discarding dried out markers and red pens left over from my early days of teaching. Wedged into the side was a card, still in its envelope. I immediately knew what it was, and rushed to reread its contents:

Mrs. Adkins!
I just wanted to thank you for your encouragement this year. You have truly made a difference in my life, and you taught me to love English again! Because God has allowed us to cross paths, I feel better prepared to go and serve in Costa Rica! Please keep being a light to those lost high schoolers. You truly make a difference.

Thank you for everything!
Sally

Sally brought that to me the Monday after her graduation, when most of her class was celebrating on the beach. I remember how touched I was that she returned to school to deliver it, how honored I was to be one of the teachers she chose to visit. The gift card she tucked inside informed me that it was, "For school supplies!" I never knew she noticed my love of pretty paperclips or, for that matter, the parts of my character that I sometimes thought of as separate from my teacher self. I bumped my podium on my way to take the computer to the cabinet, its light green background barely visible under the hundreds of signatures and notes inscribed in black permanent marker, silver paint pen and white out. Sentiments such as "Mrs. A rocks!" and "You da bomb!" made me shake my head, while the ones mentioning certain assignments or books we read or inside jokes brought back memories of certain classes that had just the right mix of personalities. Not all of those memories were pleasant, mind you, but each memory and marking represented a thread of my career up to that point, all braided and woven into a tapestry of teaching and learning, with the roles of teacher and learner often blurred. I had hoped for a job where I could impact lives, never realizing how much those lives would impact me.

I didn't revisit the last note until late that night, when I pulled it from the bathroom drawer where it had lived for eight years, a place where I could quickly access it on those days when I needed a little pick me up to get going. The tiny square of notebook paper had been folded and refolded so many times that it would no longer lie flat, and a fine layer of blush and eye shadow dust covered its outside.

Dear Mrs. Adkins,

Thank you for not being a jerk like most other teachers. I really appreciate how you have tried to help me, even if I didn't take advantage of your offer to let me make my work up. If I could, I would do it over again. It might seem weird me writing you but I always write my teachers I like. You're only the third teacher I've actually liked enough to thank. Well, class is almost over so I'll let you go. Just remember always that you are a great teacher, and you picked the right career. I hope that you don't get old and mean like so many other teachers.

Most thankfully,
Matthew

And there it was: affirmation that I was doing what I was meant to do. And that affirmation means so much more to me than the "Thanks for all you do" messages my principal scrawls on the bottom of memos mentioning an upcoming conference where I am presenting. It means more to me than the "Teacher of the Year" award I've never gotten, an award voted on by the faculty who really have no way of knowing what happens in other teachers' classrooms. And it means more to me than the N.D.D. emblazoned on the value added report that acts as a "thumbs up, a way to go" on the status quo. These notes from my students, beyond their ability to make me smile on a bad day, are evidence in writing that I have impacted their lives. The difference might not always have been detectable in test scores or grades or even classroom behavior, but what I say and how I act matters. And, if a student remembers that, and gains a love of learning for having entered my classroom though they forget every convention, literary term and short story I taught them, well, I can live with that.

Heather Adkins received a B.A. and M.A. in English from Western Kentucky University. As a student teacher in 2002, she was assigned to Gallatin High School in Gallatin, Tennessee, and has continued teaching there since that time. She teaches 11th and 12th grade English and creative writing and sponsors the creative writing club. She is an adjunct instructor at Volunteer State Community College. Her work as teacher consultant and technology liaison with the Middle Tennessee Writing Project provides her the opportunity to work with teachers of writing across Middle Tennessee and to grow the reach of the site through the implementation of technology initiatives. Much of her writing focuses on place and is inspired by life in the country with her husband and daughte

Spelling Kansas

Arica Carlson

After finishing two years at a community college, I was thrust into public school to refine my interpreting skills for deaf and hard of hearing students. The powers that be sent me to a middle school. And I hated middle schoolers almost as much as I hated my experience in middle school. Middle schoolers loved to prove authority wrong and, when they could, they smugly relished it. I was about to turn twenty. I was inexperienced. I was young. I was intimidated. That year I learned that twelve is the cut-off age for hugs.

I worked with about six kids, including Crystal. She was twelve and feisty, but she was smart, too. She had a sassy pre-teen attitude. She was precisely the reason I loathed middle school age students. She fought with her classmates, tossed her attitude around to her interpreters and her teachers, and was often in trouble for one thing or another. When I started, her interpreters were trying to break Crystal from the hugging ritual. As an elementary student, it is acceptable to hug your interpreters as you greeted them every morning, just like a kindergartener who hugs his teacher. Unfortunately, for Crystal, middle school meant hugging interpreters was not only discouraged, the interpreters considered it downright disrespectful. Fresh from college, I didn't see anything wrong with hugging. Crystal was Deaf. Deaf people hug. Hugging is a Deaf cultural norm. But the interpreters with whom I worked contended she was now too old to be hugging adults in a professional setting such as school. What did I know? I had no experience. Who was I to say otherwise?

As someone so new to sign language, I often had trouble understanding what the kids were saying. Sometimes I even played along like I knew what they were saying, nodding like another hearing idiot. Their hands would come at me like a surging tide, overwhelming me and causing my brain to choke. It wasn't until I responded incorrectly that they were on to me. One day, Crystal approached me and asked me how to spell K-S. I was confused. Who was K-S? I had heard of this before that deaf children often assumed we interpreters knew everyone they knew. "How do you spell K-S?" she asked me again, giving me that "duh, I'm waiting" look that was often on her face.

I didn't know who K-S was. I asked her again. "Who was K-S?" She huffed air at me, her bangs flipping up in a puff, then pursed her lips. Then she signed, "I'm fed up with you," as if she was my mother and walked away.

She approached another interpreter, and it wasn't until I heard that interpreter begin spelling out loud that I understood what Crystal was asking. "K-A-N-S-A-S." Kansas was often shortened to K-S. Oh. I was crestfallen. A twelve year-old girl had just made me feel like a lousy interpreter and an even crummier human being. I finished my practicum there and vowed to never interpret in a middle school again.

As I was finishing up my fourth year of interpreting, I took the opportunity to interpret at a summer camp for deaf and hard of hearing kids. I thought it would be fun to get paid to play, as I hadn't been to camp during my own childhood. The first day I was assigned to the lice check table, so I got to meet everyone incoming. That's when I saw her. Crystal. She was now sixteen and she looked more like a woman than a grumpy, disagreeable kid. Her hair had grown out long and wavy, she wore glasses, she had curves. And she actually smiled at people. She passed me by without a second glance.

It would be my luck that I would be the interpreter assigned to her cabin. As the week went on, it was obvious she didn't remember me the sharp way I remembered her. Her insolence towards adults had made me stick to high school education ever since working with her. On the third night, a war amongst the cabin girls had broken out. Crystal was crying. The counselors and I were called to meet with Crystal to see what had started the fight. As I interpreted the conversation between her and her Deaf counselor, a full spectrum picture of Crystal's life came into focus. She was sobbing, her hands shaking as words came off them. The girls were teasing her and spreading rumors. I could hear my voice saying her words, explaining her rickety home life, in and out of her mother's house. She was still just a kid. It dawned on me: she had been going through this just as she was getting to middle school. The attitude, the trouble with friends, and the massive amount of disrespect for adults were symptoms of a life she was struggling to live. It all made sense now, four years later. And the safe adults at school took away her hugs during a time when maybe no one else was hugging her.

The next day, we tested our courage on a ropes course. Two hundred feet in the air, we were each harnessed in and challenged to walk a tight rope with only one parallel rope as our support. Crystal bravely volunteered to be first. I watched from the ground, interpreting the advice and encouragement from her ropes coach. One foot slipped from the single wire, but she juggled her weight, ripped with her arms, and miraculously regained her balance. Tears sprung suddenly into my eyes as I watched Crystal conquer the tightrope obstacle despite almost falling. Back on the ground, she held her hands out to show me how badly she was shaking. She was smiling. I was too.

The next morning at breakfast, I confessed my secret to Crystal. "Do you remember me?" I asked. "I was a student interpreter at your middle school a few years ago."

Her eyes lit up as recognition finally hit her. "I knew your face," Crystal signed to me. She smiled like we were long lost pals.

The last day of camp kids scurried around autographing each other's memory books and taking last minute goofy pictures. They traded books back and forth, perching on any table, hill or rock large enough to sit down and write a message. As they chased each other for signatures and socialized for the last time of the summer, I stood supervising on a grassy hill. Crystal approached me with her book.

"Will you sign my book?" she asked me, almost shyly.

"Sure," I said with a shrug. I sat down with the book propped up on my knees and began to write. "So fun to see you again," I wrote. Lame! I paused, trying to find what I really wanted to say. My mind was stuck on four years ago. Perhaps no one had ever told her what a brat she was back then: how awful she was to everyone around her, how she treated the adults and her classmates, how crummy she made me feel when she didn't give me a second chance at understanding what she was saying.

I posed the pen, ready to write. Then my mind flashed back to the three of us sitting at a weathered picnic bench while she cried and dumped out her life in front of us. Her words drifted back through my head. She was a miserable kid because she was miserable. But she wasn't broken by her experiences. She still smiled. She still found joy. She conquered the struggle of building a new life like she tenaciously conquered the high wire. What I took as a sassy pre-teen attitude was the hardening shell of a very scared, lonely child. She was so different now. Then I wrote something I thought she needed to read. To say something maybe no one had said to her before.

"It has been such a pleasure to see what a bright, courageous, open-minded young woman you are becoming," I wrote the final line in her book.

About six months later, I attended a theatre event that was being performed in sign language. It was only natural that all the deaf and hard of hearing kids from the entire state would be there. As I approached the front doors with my family, I was nearly bowled over from the side in a hug. When I turned to look, my eyes met Crystal's, blue and shining behind her glasses. I threw my arms around her and hugged her back firmly. Twelve is *not* the cut off age for hugs.

Arica Carlson has a B.S. in education from the University of Nebraska at Omaha and an associate degree in interpreting from Iowa Western Community College. She has been working with high school students with hearing loss for six years. Although she has ventured into other types of interpreting, including religious and video relay, educational interpreting has grown deep roots in her heart. She currently works in a secondary setting in the Omaha metro area where she lives with her husband and new son. Many years ago, her English teacher recommended her for a summer honors writing program. She has been writing ever since. Her previous works have appeared in the *Anthology of Poetry by Young Americans* and *Illuminations*.

When the Roots are Still Alive

Jennifer Ernsthausen

A year ago, I became a gardener. I did not decide willingly, but circumstances dragged me into it. Before this, all my friends and family knew that if you gave me a plant, chances were that it would die. I had proved this again and again. Over time, I decided that I couldn't grow plants. When I bought a rambling old duplex, I settled for planting shrubs that flowered each spring. Trim them once a year. Water them occasionally. Mission accomplished. I wasn't trying to create something horticulturally extraordinary. Mediocre was an accomplishment for me.

At the beginning of the summer of 2010, my dearest friend showed up with a van full of potted flowers. Her family had been transferred across the country, and she was bringing me her beautiful flowers; there were varieties I didn't know existed, let alone understand how to care for. I looked at the twenty or so pots and felt overwhelmed and helpless. A long page of instructions for each plant was meant to ease my mind. It told me when to feed them, what to feed them, how much to feed them. Four plants died within two weeks. Discouraged, I consulted the instructions again. Each empty pot was a marker of my failure. I decided to go online and do a little research. I discovered that I needed to do move some plants out of direct sunlight. When leaves droop, the plant is thirsty. When the leaves go yellow and limp, they are over-saturated with water. This was not anywhere on my instruction sheet. Eventually, I began to learn through my mistakes.

It was then that I realized that this gardening journey is similar to the one I am taking to become an effective teacher. Staring at those languishing plants, feeling overwhelmed, was not unlike my first day in front of my classroom, fresh out of college. What do I do? What happens if I fail? Can they tell I don't know what I'm doing?

Reading over the pages of plant care instructions was not unlike the lesson plans and curriculum pages I pored over, hoping for some brilliant insight that would provide instant success. Instant success was not forthcoming. As a new teacher, I thought good teaching was doing everything the curriculum said to do. The curriculum didn't tell me how to stop Jasmine from walking out of class or make Wallace accountable for doing his homework. There were no next steps when a third of the class bombed the test. Students are as diverse as the multitude of flowers in a garden. There is no one, guaranteed successful way to reach all students; there was no comprehensive list of instructions.

Different students require different approaches. I learned through reflecting on my failures. What went wrong? What went right? What can I try differently? What does the research say? What do my students say? What do I say that brightens their faces? What do I say that makes their shoulders droop?

As I learned how to keep my plants alive, something unexpected happened. I began to love plants. I started to add to my collection. My plants were living rather than drooping, and my confidence began to build. I decided to expand and try my hand at outside gardening. I planted some seeds. I watered them and celebrated when little green leaves pushed out of the soil. The plants didn't flower. I religiously gave them Miracle Gro. When my mom visited, I proudly showed off my plants that were growing from seed. I was mortified when my mom identified them as weeds. I had the healthiest weeds in the neighborhood. The problem was that I didn't know what weeds looked like and how to tell the difference. It was green. It was growing. It must be good.

A similar thing happened in my classroom. When I began teaching writing, I thought poetry had to be exact. My students produced a set of boring, short, unimaginative poems. The children had worked hard and finished the project with no spelling mistakes. Each poem followed the model. Therefore, it must be good. But, even as a novice teacher, I recognized that the poems were not inspiring or descriptive. They did not paint pictures in one's mind or rivet the listener. Poetry was supposed to be beautiful and poignant. My students' poetry was neither. I decided that I was a terrible writing teacher; teaching poetry was too tough for third graders, and, perhaps, I should avoid poetry altogether. Online resources were not helpful. Books made it seem simple which in turn made me feel irritatingly inept. The actual problem was that I was teaching students to write poetry when I hated poetry and couldn't write it myself. I didn't know what poetry was.

I figured that sooner or later my principal was going to discover my lousy poetry teaching skills, so I signed myself up for the Western Pennsylvania Writing Project. That summer I learned to love to write. I experienced first hand the struggle a writer engages in as she attempts to channel memories, emotions, and opinions into compelling phrases. I learned what poetry was and how to grow writers. We began to explore words and play with them. We practiced describing things we could not touch, see, or hear. Most of all, we found a way to put the fleeting pictures from our minds on paper and stretch them out. My students' poetry became beautiful and poignant. I proudly posted it in the hallway. Teachers would stop by and say, "There is no way Ramon wrote that. He is in special ed. He can't even read." Ramon's poem started with, "Sadness sounds like the dripping of a thousand faucets, one drip at a time." He may not have been able to read, but he had wonderful words inside his head, waiting to find a way out. I discovered that my development as a teacher is similar to my development as a gardener. I needed to *know* it to *grow* it.

In the past, when an unfortunate plant started to wither or go brown, I would put it in a grocery bag and put it at the bottom of my trash pail. Another one down. Another failure. I knew to never buy *that kind* of plant again. Lately, I have been taking brown leaves as a challenge. Brown leaves can mean hopeful instead of hopeless. I move these feeble plants to a new location and see what happens. I change the way I water them and see what happens. I give them double Miracle-Gro, trim off the dead leaves, and see what happens. I currently have six such challenges on my back porch. I get such pleasure out of seeing them grow a new green leaf or push up a bud.

I am ashamed to admit that I used to view my students, who were rough around the edges or low achieving, as potential failures. But I now know that it was my failure, not my students'. I have started seeing such challenging children as opportunities for growth. A few years ago, one of my students, Jasmine, would last about half a period or so before overturning her chair and walking out. I would dread the moment she would leave and the distraction it always caused, but a piece of me felt that now I could focus on the other students with her gone. Half way through the year, I realized that I was not taking responsibility for educating her, and I was allowing her behavior to justify not being accountable to her. I decided to change. Instead of hoping Jasmine would leave sooner than later, I began to challenge myself to see how long I could engage her to stay. I stopped viewing her as the problem and started viewing her as part of my team. I put her name in the challenge problem, which we did not discuss until the end of class. She decided to stick around to see the answer and check if she was right. I knew Jasmine was much brighter than her tests showed, so I paired her up with a struggling student. Jasmine loved to talk and boss others around, and I looked for a way for that to happen in a positive manner. Jasmine stopped walking out of my class regularly, and she raised her grade from a D+ to a B-.

I have learned to stubbornly believe that there is hope, even when the dry, brown leaves tell another story. Often the root is still alive. I have had plants that looked dead but grew again the next year to my great surprise. I have been paying special attention to my resurrected snowball bush, and this year it is green and healthy.

This renaissance can happen in teaching, too. One fond memory is of my former student, Antonio. At the beginning of the year, I was told he was a behavior problem and would do no work. The first day, Antonio lived up to his reputation. By lunch, I decided to call home. I asked his grandmother if I could keep him after school until his work was completed. She agreed. When the other students left, and Antonio realized couldn't leave until his work was complete, he got to it. I discovered he was very smart. He did a day's work in an hour or so. There were bumpy days when he tried to outmaneuver me, but Antonio never missed a day of school that year, even on snow days when his bus did not come. He walked the two miles to be in school. He wrote beautiful poems and read them in an oddly deep baritone voice for a third grader. He discovered that he loved the spotlight and spent months turning a short story into a play, which he helped direct. Antonio had a love of learning buried deep beneath his "I don't care" attitude.

Two years ago, I could count the plants in and around my house on one hand. Today, I have a yearly spring flower budget, and I have over a hundred plants. Blooms and green leaves surround me. I am just an average gardener and still have much to learn. I find myself noticing gardens everywhere. I take pictures, and I am planning to have an even better garden next year.

I am also still learning to be an effective teacher. In every school and classroom I visit and work, I notice new ideas, cultures, strategies, and approaches. Conversations with other teachers spark new plans. Next year is going to be better even if this year was already great. Each spring starts with bare earth that promotes endless possibilities of garden configurations. Each fall starts with a fresh class of children. Anything is possible. In my journey, as a teacher and gardener, I have learned that failure is just the beginning of worthwhile inquiry.

Jennifer **Ernsthausen** received her B. A. from Trent University, Ontario, Canada, and her B. Ed. from Brock University, Ontario, Canada. Upon moving to Pennsylvania, she received her gifted teaching certificate from Chatham University and completed the Writing Project Institute at the University of Pittsburgh. Jennifer has taught third grade for most of her sixteen years with the Pittsburgh Public School District. She currently teaches third grade math, and, as editor of the school's newspaper, she continues to foster writers and dabble in writing.

Getting Someplace

Kate Kennedy

Several weeks ago, sorting through milk crates loaded with teaching materials, I unearthed a manila folder labeled "Basic Writing." Inside it were emails I'd written to my husband in the spring semester of 2000 when my planning period happened to be scheduled right after basic writing class. Designed as a remedial course for tenth through twelfth graders, Basic Writing had morphed over the years. It had become both proving ground and dumping ground. Recently mainstreamed English learners signed up, as did native speakers, including ninth graders. Ours was a crazy community, a collision of language, culture, religion, and social class, not to mention age, attitude, and personality. In other words, it was my favorite class.

About half my students had come to the U.S. as refugees or immigrants from Somalia, Sudan, Cambodia, Vietnam, Eritrea, El Salvador, Bosnia, Russia, and Afghanistan. The rest were Mainers, born and bred. Our common ground? Everyone struggled to write with coherence, confidence, and fluidity. Some had practiced writing in English only a little. The children of war or poverty or repression, some lacked formal schooling in any language. The Maine-born kids had failed to hop aboard the writing train for varied (and often overlapping) reasons themselves: a learning disability or illness or truancy or behavior troubles or trauma. Two academically focused Bosnians simply needed to burnish their verbs.

In class, a number of girls wore head-scarves; others wore tight, low-cut tee-shirts. A boy from Vietnam used one hand to type because of a stroke; a Somali boy suffered from what I think might now be diagnosed as P.T.S.D. Two sixteen year-old girls, one Afghani, one Cambodian, were already married.

Here are some excerpts from the folder labeled "Basic Writing" during our labors on writing personal narratives—stories from our lives. I've changed names, but, otherwise, kept these emails as I found them, full of disarray, yes, as well as a little humble lift-off.

***

February 15, 2000

We talked about scary experiences today, leading up to writing one. Mary Jackson told us about needing back surgery when she was ten, and how, ever since she woke up from the anesthetic, she has at odd moments thought maybe her real life is a dream she's not yet woken from.

February 17, 2000

Jimmy Im was back. Three absences already. Jimmy's got cool slicked back hair, gangsta pants. He's Cambodian. Lots of beautiful gold jewelry around his neck, including a large jade tooth-shaped pendant. When we did idea webbing about scary times in their lives (groans from the kids but they're good-natured), I walked around helping and checking papers. In the center of Jimmy's circle sat the word "dream". His story: his mom dreamed that his little brother was shot by a stranger in their backyard. The next day she told him not to play in the yard. Of course he did. Later that day, Jimmy heard a gunshot: a man firing, though nobody hurt. "What my mom dreams, come true," he said.

"She has a gift," I said.

"Yes, a gift."

Ali 's circle contained the word "lion". Back in Somalia, a lion had once walked into his bedroom. It was not a roaring, scary lion, more of a pet, but he didn't know this at the time. So, that one morning, when he was a young boy, he woke to find the lion watching him sleep.

Two Portland-born 9th graders wrote about pregnancy scares. One of them, Tammy, wrote a piece today about a girl living on the streets—five lines, difficult to decipher for the spelling and syntax errors, but a resounding message. I got it.

February 28, 2000

I gave a three-sentence dictation at the beginning of class. Unusual for me to do that, but I'd told everybody, repeatedly—begged them—

that at least they had to spell "Basic Writing" correctly. Then we wandered into the murkier terrain of "written" and "writer".

1.   I am excited about writing.
2.   Today I have written two letters.
3.   Being a writer is hard and interesting.

Lots of creative variations. The Bosnians spelled everything right. Otherwise, it's a mixed bag… The feeling today after vacation was pretty good, glad-to-see-each-other, and productive. I know I looked forward to seeing them. As usual, after a traumatic beginning to the semester, they've won my heart.

March 1, 2000

Before the kids wrote on computers, I handed back their dictations, then asked everyone to go to the chalkboards (one had **WRITTEN** at the top, the second, **WRITER**, the third, **WRITING**). "Okay," I said, "copy the word at the top of your board five times, then go on to the next." (They do this sort of thing happily—moving around, jostling, laughing.) Joseph from Sudan, careful with handwriting, had already printed five lovely versions of **WITING** before I pointed out the missing R and he corrected them. Sigh. Tammy's efforts were so messy only I could read them.

Then it was on to the overhead projector—red erasable marker. "Okay," I said, "we need a guinea pig." Briana volunteered. "Even without knowing what for?" I asked.

"Sure," she said.

"Okay, you're to tell us about some *first time* experience: first time driving, first day of school, first moments in the US, first day of a new job, first time you fell in love [dangerous terrain], first time you felt grownup, first whatever. We're going to imagine that Briana's planning to write a paper about a first time, and we're going to look at how she might write her introduction."

"Snowboarding for the first time," she said.

"Okay," I asked, "what goes in the introduction?"

"The body?" said Tammy.

"No," I said, "that comes after the introduction."

The body—haha. Jimmy Im and Sam Nguyen exchanged rib punches.

Finally, we had a subject and some sort of reaction to it on the overhead transparency: *The first time I went snowboarding was last year at Sunday River. Although it was hard at first, I grew to like it a lot.*

"Is it my turn yet?" asked Janice. "Mine's about my friend who liked a guy for the first time, but he already had 5,000 girlfriends—"

"You're sure this is okay for school?" I asked.

"Oh, yeah. Nothin happened. Well, he had like five girlfriends, and she's like I want to be the only one, and he's like—"

"And what was her overall reaction to this?" I asked.

"She hated guys. They're so cruel. They do you dirt like they're so mean."

"You sound like a country-western song," I said.

Janice's introduction went something like this: *My friend—I'm callin her Amber—she liked a boy for the first time, but it ended up she hated men.*

After vainly trying to wrap things up, we hit the computers. I told the group they hadn't worked very hard last time, so let's get cracking. Everybody but Brianna seemed to get somewhere. She claimed a "brain cramp". After the usual chaos, the room settled down, more or less. Tanya from Bosnia wanted to know the difference between "live" and "leave". I gave her examples, then we talked about the difference in pronunciation. She practiced, laughing at the unfamiliar way her lips moved.

No "Santana"-listening for Jimmy Im. I said he had to finish his piece this class period. He worked hard and was finally able to print something out. A big deal.

May 2, 2000

Today, somehow, we all muddled through. I showed two papers on the overhead projector: Zara's (Somali-born), and Joanne's (Maine-born). They like that. Then computer problems. Finally Mary said, "These computers su—. I ain't working any more." I agreed, said okay, and that was that. Luckily, not much time left in class. Usually, Mary's one of my helpers. Ali spaced out and never got to the computer. Jimmy couldn't log in. But I did get to sit beside Brianna and help her, as well spend some time with Juan. In the midst of this, two kids went to the cafeteria and came back with French fries, ketchup and a clear plastic tray of nachos—corn chips beside a pool of *Easy Cheese*. Miriam dipped a chip in, then made a face, ran over to the wastebasket, and spit out her nacho. Quite a picture, Miriam in her long flowered skirt and head-scarf and fleece jacket.

Basically, I believe the kids do more work when I let them go to the lav and the caf. But sometimes I have to say, "Straighten up, it's too much like a lounge in here!" They do make me laugh, and I do think they're getting someplace, just not where I imagined they might go. They continue to train me.

***

When I originally sent these e-mail messages home, I imagined that analyzing them would help me improve my teaching. Maybe it did. But now, on rereading them eleven years after-the-fact, it's the Basic Writers themselves who shine: their scrappiness and humor, the poignancy of their lives, their willingness to try, to trust, and what I can only call their grace. It wasn't pretty. In fact, it was a mess. A mess with meaning, I believe.

Since 2006, **Kate Kennedy** has been the director of the Southern Maine Writing Project at the University of Southern Maine. She taught writing at Portland High School in Portland, Maine, for twenty years and has also taught basic literacy, sudden fiction, and E.S.L. to adults. Her novel, *End Over End*, was published by Soho Press in 2001. A book of short biographies, *More than Petticoats: Remarkable Maine Women*, came out in 2005 from Globe Pequot Press. She has published short fiction and nonfiction as well as edited novels and a guidebook. Kate received a B.A. in French literature from Wellesley College and an M.A. in teaching English as a second language from U.C.L.A. Although she grew up in California and New Jersey, Maine has been her home since 1977. She and her husband, Nate Greene, live in Cape Elizabeth, enjoying three generations of family within a sixty-five mile span.

The Aftertaste of Testing
(after Sandra Cisneros' "Eleven")

Kathleen Hicks

What they never tell you about teaching is that when you're a teacher, you're also a college student and a high school student and a middle school kid and a grade school baby and somebody's daughter before all of that. And, when you wake up in the morning you expect to feel like a teacher, but you don't. It feels like every other day. And you don't feel different at all, just layers of paint, color after color, on the same old piece of furniture.

One day there's a fight in your classroom, and you watch your hands protecting students while calling security and soaking up blood, and you realize you're a teacher. Then you make hurt puppy sounds and cry on the drive home because it's so sad and that part of you is a grade school baby. Then you research to find out why it happened and that's your college self. You talk about it with your friends, and your middle school self camps out in your mouth for the rest of the day. That's what I tell myself when I creep home to my mother. I need to be a daughter, and that's fine, too.

Sometimes, I feel like being a teacher isn't enough. I want to be an ancient principal in charge of the whole school, one who has seen everything before and could snap her fingers and make everyone and everything behave and be happy. Say "stop" and all the problems would sit down. Then I realize it wouldn't feel any different than today in some ways. Some days, I think it would be easier to give my teacher self a thick shell of protection and courage, so no one will see they have chipped some of my paint away.

And what they don't understand about teaching is that you're a teacher every day, even when the students leave.

On the day all students who passed the California High School Exit Exam (CAHSEE) went to Magic Mountain, students swaggered up and down the halls, back and forth in their "I survived CAHSEE" shirts and dark, crisp blue jeans that still had fold lines in them from the store. It smelled like Cool Water cologne, and Aqua Net left a visible cloud in the air. Tenth graders chugged soda at eight in the morning to lull their rumbling stomachs through the long bus ride and a day without free lunch. Excitement sparkled in the air. I was a teacher and so proud of the young scholars who jumped the first of many hurdles before their diplomas.

I led my students into my classroom and felt the room vibrate with joy. All I had to do was take roll then release them to the busses waiting outside. This was my honors class—my only honors class at the time—and almost every single student passed the CAHSEE. They planned to ride roller coasters until they threw up and miss school for a day without any consequences. At that moment, I knew what I was doing.

My day unraveled when there was only one student left. He missed passing the English section of the CAHSEE by two points. His best friend walked out the classroom door. Then his seatmate followed. Eventually, the rest of the kids that he had spent the last eleven years following all left. He was alone. I could see it hurt. I didn't see what came next.

"This is all your fault," he said, his trusting brown eyes looking straight into mine.

His voice was steady and sure. I felt my body shrink down, down, down into my clothes and suddenly my shoes and pants and sweater felt too big. Then, I wasn't just the teacher, but also the college student who said the wrong thing and the high school girl with mismatched clothes and the middle school kid who was too small to play sports and the grade school baby teased for being blonde and a daughter falling hard off of a curb onto the concrete sidewalk. He was wrong, but it didn't make it hurt any less.

What they don't tell you about teaching and what you don't realize is that becoming a teacher isn't finishing a college class or getting a square hat with a tassel on it or even standing in front of a classroom full of students. It's when someone says, "It's your fault," and you say, "I am so sorry you can't go. Let's work on this together."

And you remind yourself that he is hurting to his core. Then you know protecting his layers is just as important as protecting your own.

Kathleen Hicks received a B.A. from California Lutheran University and a M.Ed. from the University of California, Los Angeles. She facilitates a writing pedagogy course at a local university and is a fellow through U.C.L.A.'s Writing Project while continuing to doggy paddle through her third year of teaching remedial language arts, English 10, advanced placement language and composition, and acting as department chair in South Los Angeles at Ánimo Locke 1, a school specializing in supporting English language learners. Other things she enjoys are: engaging students in critical discussions regarding oppression, advocating for students' rights in urban schools, and dodge ball. (What other sport requires a person to apologize after she whacks someone in the face? If you can answer, please, let her know. She would play that sport, too.) Her poetry has appeared in *Morning Glory* and *The Word*, both published through California Lutheran University.

Doing Time in American Lit

Mary Kistel

Today I stand outside my door and ask students to draw a character's name from *The Great Gatsby* out of a plastic bag as they enter my class. Some grimace, some giggle, but most are curious: what will she make us do with this character? Sean, however, is hostile. He glares at me when he chooses the female character, Jordan Baker, and begrudgingly takes his seat as the bell rings. We have just read the first five chapters of the novel, and I ask students to write an analysis of the character they chose showing his or her personality through story details. I also ask them to choose a symbol and a color to define their character. Sean's hand shoots up in the air, and, when I call on him, his voice is full of resentment.

"I have no idea what you're talking about."

I exhale quietly before I answer. "Why don't you come see me during tutorial after school?"

Sean rolls his eyes, and that's that.

* * *

It's 3:05 pm—tutorial ended 5 minutes ago, but Sean persists. His jaws clench, as his nervous left foot pounds the carpet of my classroom. He wants out of here, but he's a disciplined athlete who's made up his mind to stay no matter what—until he understands his homework. He tries to capture my advice in his own personal short hand.

"OK, fine, you want a symbol—Jordan Baker is a golf pro—how about a golf club?"

I smile. When I collect these paragraphs tomorrow, I will find that most Jordan Baker symbols will be golf clubs. Sean's a practical young man and resents me asking him to go into detail; he's been on *the-least-I-need-to-know-to-get-a-B-so-I-can-get-a-baseball-scholarship-and-get-out-of-here* plan, but his lack of effort hasn't met his own standards. He's got to raise his grades. You know when you irritate someone, and I irritate Sean. After several "incidents" in the middle of class where Sean accused me of grading unfairly because he didn't understand and my reminding him that I offer tutorial after school every day, he's finally shown up, and we have some one-on-one time. This time is important.

"That symbol works. So what color do you think symbolizes Jordan Baker?"

"That part's easy—I already know what I'm doing for that."

"Really?" Now I was curious.

"Yeah, I chose gray for Jordan Baker. Remember when we read that story? I think it was *The Red Badge of Courage*, and that Crane guy said the sharp shooter had gray eyes and the guy remembered that gray-eyed people had better vision?"

I was shocked. He was wrong—that tidbit came from Ambrose Bierce—but the actual incident was correct, and he remembered something from a reading in first semester—not the norm at the end of second semester. I noticed for the first time that Sean had gray eyes.

"Wonderful, Sean! That's from the Civil War story we read right before *The Red Badge of Courage*. Do you remember 'An Occurrence at Owl Creek Bridge'?"

"Oh yeah, the story about that guy who's gonna be hanged."

"That's the one. So why do you choose gray for Jordan?"

"Well, it says she has gray eyes. I think she sees things. She knows Tom Buchanan is cheating on his wife, 'cuz Jordan talks about it to Nick. I know she lies and cheats at golf and everything, but she's out to protect herself. That's why she sees things."

I was floored. I had never heard such a deep insight from this student before. "You have got to share this in class tomorrow—so everyone can hear this connection—it's incredible! Would you mind sharing it?"

Sean actually grinned at me. "I can, if you want me to."

* * *

Sean smiles at me again as he enters class. Before I collect the paragraphs, I tell my students that they will be creating a literature quilt, and the details they came up with last night will help them make squares that will be tied together to hang in our room. The quilt is based on the idea that F. Scott Fitzgerald gives us a glimpse into windows of wealth in the 1920's, and they will write about what they see when they look in those windows. The color they chose for their character will be the color of their square. Although they need to finish reading the novel before they can really begin to work on this project, I want them thinking about it as they read.

I glance at Sean before I continue, and he nods. "Sean saw something last night that I'd like him to share with you."

Sean looks around hesitantly and clears his throat. "Well, I just thought about that hanging story we read about the Civil War and how gray-eyed people see better. And since Jordan Baker has gray eyes, I thought it was kind of weird that she's the one who told Nick about Tom cheating—it's like she sees things. She knows what's going on and how to protect herself, 'cuz she's dating a nice guy like Nick."

"Isn't that a great observation?" I ask, looking for support. "I never would have made that connection between 'An Occurrence at Owl Creek Bridge' and *The Great Gatsby*."

Emma's excited and raises her hand enthusiastically. "Oh my gosh, that is so awesome! Couldn't we make every Jordan Baker square gray? I mean what other color could it be after that detail? I think they've got to be gray!"

Chris slams his fist on the desk, and thumps Sean on the back. "That's it, bro, gray squares for Jordan."

Three linebackers in the back row start chanting, "Gray-Squares! Jor-dan! Gray-Squares! Jor-dan!"

Across the room, Sean's gray eyes shine.

Mary Kistel, an Air Force brat, spent many years growing up in England where her father served three tours of duty. She received a B.A. in English from Furman University and an M.A.T. from Florida Gulf Coast University. She has taught middle school in Southwest Florida, and is a teacher consultant for the National Writing Project at FGCU. She was a panelist for the standard-setting meeting of the 2011 National Assessment of Education Progress for writing. She currently teaches British literature and senior English at Bishop Verot Catholic High School in Fort Myers, Florida, where she lives with her husband and Sheltie. She has a married daughter and a son who plays college football.

Teaching Means Realizing Potential

Hidden Potential

Steve Massart

The glowing tip of his cigarette seemed to light the narrow, smoky office as much as the dim desk lamp. I sat in the hard wooden chair, looking out the window and wishing I could join the hazy late-evening sun in its retreat. A student rarely finds a summons to the principal's office a pleasant affair. So, it is with similar trepidation that a soldier finds an order to report to his commander. But for the third time in a matter of a few weeks, I found myself sitting in the cramped office trying to avoid the stare of the staff sergeant who was my instructor at the non-commissioned officer academy. Instead of looking into his eyes, I alternately watched the sunset and the glowing tip of the cigarette that he constantly lifted to his lips and waited for him to break the thick silence and speak.

***

Staff Sergeant Carver smoked too much, drank twice that, and looked nothing like the fit, focused, and fearless soldiers in the ads my Army recruiter used to convince me to enlist toward the end of my senior year of high school. Sergeant Carver looked liked he had a perpetual hangover, hadn't shaved in days, and wore uniforms that hadn't ever seen an iron. His appearance seemed to explain why he had almost twenty years of service to my two, but only outranked me by one stripe.

He carried the weight of his hidden wounds in his narrow shoulders. You could hear it during class in the way his voice drifted mid-sentence, his focus drawn away by memories too demanding to ignore. The residual alcohol made the first hours of the day lighter for him, but an hour or two before he released us for lunch, words started to retreat, and the ones he did find seemed somehow heavier, like their component syllables had just finished a long march through an even longer night.

The other instructors in the school, some of whom outranked Staff Sergeant Carver, would have completely dismissed him as a burnout save for one embroidered patch he wore on his uniform: the rifle surrounded by a wreath of leaves—the Combat Infrantryman Badge. The patch symbolized his sacrifice not in a peacetime army like the other instructors but in combat.

***

The first time Staff Sergeant Carver summoned me to his office, I expected to be reprimanded for doing little more than meeting the bare minimums in class and around the barracks. With only nine months left in the service, I hadn't wanted to attend the non-commissioned officer academy—the month-long basic training for soldiers who were about to be promoted to the rank of sergeant. Despite my repeated and lengthy appeals for someone else to attend in my place, my captain ordered me to go. I did but with little motivation and one heck of a begrudging attitude—just like my approach had been to middle and high school, which is what had landed me in front of a military recruiter instead of a college admissions administrator in the first place.

But, instead of the expected reprimand, Sergeant Carver informed me that he was promoting me to cadet first sergeant, meaning I would be in charge of over three hundred soldiers for the last week of our training cycle. I don't know if it ever dawned on him that most of the cadets were older than me, outranked me, and had many more years of service, not to mention much better attitudes. He didn't ask me whether or not I wanted the job; he simply said through a cloud of cigarette smoke, "I think you've got what it takes." At my second summons, I expected to be reprimanded for doing something wrong as cadet first sergeant, but he informed me that at the end of the training cycle, each instructor nominated one soldier to compete for the Distinguished Soldier Award and that I was his nominee.

***

Sergeant Carver summoned me for the third and final time, as I completed my evening rounds of the barracks. Just hours before, I had competed for and won the leadership award, but the way Sergeant Carver's eyes met me at the door filled me with trepidation. He seemed both pleased with me and yet somehow angry. I looked past him and alternately watched the sunset and the glowing tip of his cigarette.

Long, silent minutes passed before he finally spoke. And when he did, it wasn't to congratulate me on the leadership award but to start telling stories of his three tours in Vietnam as an artilleryman. As he talked, he pointed at the fifty or more framed pictures of men, machines, and foreign landscapes covering the long narrow walls. Of the fears that arrived at night, the rocket attacks, the men he'd lost, pouring motor oil into machine gun chambers so they could fire nonstop at the slithering ghosts advancing through the rice paddies toward his position. Of how, when the chopper came on his 365th day—the final day of his mandatory year "in country"—he couldn't

wait to get on it and get back home. But once back in the States, he couldn't stand knowing that he'd abandoned his brothers that he'd left a mission unfinished. He volunteered for two more tours of duty in that hostile land.

The next day, after I lead the company through its graduation ceremony formation, Sergeant Carver approached me, looking as slovenly as ever despite the added pressure of the visiting dignitaries and family members. After he put a lit cigarette between his lips, he shook my hand and said, "Good work, soldier." He turned and walked back into the barracks, a ghost himself. I never saw him again.

***

I've had many fine teachers and college professors over the years, but none have impacted me as much as Staff Sergeant Carver. In the few short weeks I was his student, he transformed my generally unmotivated character by looking past my negative attitude, by recognizing my untapped strengths, by showing his faith in me, and by giving me challenging opportunities to realize my potential. And in doing so, he taught me more about what teaching means than anything I learned in my educator training program or in any professional development class I've since taken. He saw in me what I couldn't see in myself. He saw what I could be and, perhaps more importantly, what I needed to become.

Though well intentioned, I'm sure that everyone who has a say about what we do as educators creates layers of complexity that often interfere with our ability to effectively teach students. With the reams of state and district standards weighing down our desks, the diminishing budgets that increase our class sizes and resources, the seemingly endless lists of things to do—papers to grade, lessons to plan, parents to call, emails to be dealt with, meetings and conferences to attend—it is easy to lose sight of the most important mission we have as educators: to transform our students. To recognize their potential and then help them achieve it, even if—especially if—they're reluctant to do so.

***

Given how much Staff Sergeant Carver drank and smoked, it's hard to imagine that he's still alive. But every day, he stands next to me and helps me hold open the door for my students as I welcome them to class. He sits next to me when I'm talking with my most reluctant learners about their problems, interests, ambitions. He puts a hand on my shoulder when a new student shows up unexpectedly, assigned, of course, to my largest class.

And he reminds me that I shouldn't be thinking, "Not another one" but "I wonder what this student could become."

Steve Massart served in the United States Army from 1987-1990 before receiving his B.A. in humanities and a master's in teaching from Washington State University, Vancouver. He has taught junior high and high school English and writing courses for seventeen years, and he is proud to say that he has taught freshmen English every year of his career and hopes to do so until he retires. In addition to teaching ninth graders, he also teaches Advanced Placement literature and composition at Heritage High School in Vancouver, Washington, where he lives with his wife and three children. His short stories have appeared in *The First Line, Amazing Journeys,* and *The Writers Post Journal.*

The Calling

Brandy Price

I went into teaching out of fear. After watching my dad botch the beatnik path, I was petrified of the failed artist's life. Indeed, while my heart belonged to sports writing and dreams of writing for Sports Illustrated, my mind steered me to teaching. Teaching was my sure thing, my stable thing, my something to fall back on. Over the course of a school year, it became my *calling*.

At the tender age of twenty-two, I stood in front of a first period class of forty-seven "at risk" tenth graders. Before school starts, an administrator will generally facilitate course enrollment discussions with the school leadership team. The school leadership team will generally be made up of veteran teachers. With seemingly mathematical precision, the school leadership team will hand the "at-risk" students to the first year teachers.

This pairing usually turns on two weighty considerations; first, senior teachers do not want to deal with the behavior of "at-risk" students; second, senior teachers do not want to experience the "anchor effect" that these students have on a state standardized test scores. The latter is particularly troublesome given merit based pay schemes and performance accountability that turns almost entirely on these scores.

So, by coerced fate, there we were—the "at-risk," given up on kids and the first year teacher. "At risk" is a somewhat fancy term for students that have been allowed to habitually fail. It is a term that takes the responsibility off of teachers and education systems and places it solely on these students. In reality, we are all at risk—at risk of failing our students, of failing ourselves, and of falling even further behind in world education rankings.

My "at-risk" kids had woken up at 4:30 A.M. to board a 5:30 A.M. city bus from a neighborhood bedecked with broken bottles and bloodless yellow grass to our shiny neighborhood with vibrant trees and clean walls. They were second, third, fourth, and last chance kids. They were interlopers, visitors, trespassers, and guests. They were lost kids—tucked away in a corridor twice removed from the gleaming halls that held the academic decathletes. Their first acquaintance with their new homeland was my room—a congested and hot former storage room with fluorescent lights that blinked in an asymmetrical pattern.

Our first order of business that day was *Huck Finn*, and I had brought Garth Brooks' song *The River* to play for them; I had prepared an entire speech on the symbolic importance of the Mississippi River to the novel. I still remember Brooks' warble as he sang, "You know a dream is a like a river ever changing as it flows and the dreamer's just a vessel that must follow where it goes," and the look of horror emblazoned on the kids' faces that they realized that they were listening to country music. This was the age of the disparate voices of Tupac and No Doubt. But Brooks' voice ultimately suited us that day, and the lyrics achieved a profound eloquence over the course of the school year.

Marvin was seventeen and on his third attempt at English 10. He was the type of kid who could vanish into a shadow. He had a voice like a sparrow, slight and weak timbered. He wore a flannel shirt and jeans that were loose and clearly borrowed. The first week, he showed up twice. He stood out only because he was a beautiful writer. His journal was an eclectic compilation of jarring insights, and scribbled out philosophies. The depth of it *called* to me.

Before embarking on teaching, I was already well versed in the power of writing. I had read Rick Reilly's baseball articles, treatises on our national pastime that catapulted me back in time to a field long lost to age, into moments of elegant American history. I had read Wordsworth's *I Wandered Lonely as a Cloud* just after my grandma had passed and found comfort in his daffodils. Writing was company to my elegiac contemplations and to my joy; it is equally gracious in both.

So, I wrote to Marvin. I took my pen to the confidential canvas of his journal. In its margins, I cajoled, pushed, and questioned him. I challenged him. I celebrated him. I believed in him. I found ways to tell him about Paramount, a city so seemingly uncouth that my high school could not find teachers. I told him about the drive by shooting that punctuated my senior year and the friend who fell to gunfire at a fast food restaurant. "They wanted his boom box," I wrote.

Slowly, Marvin began to turn around. He showed up to class almost every day, and he was often early. I discovered that he had four brothers. Mom had died of cancer. Dad worked three jobs to support the family. Most of the time, Marvin went to sleep to the insistent buzz of police helicopters and barking dogs.

Without much warning, Marvin became one of my top students; he asked me to recommend him for honors English. He was too good for a first year teacher at that point. I like to think—perhaps grandiosely—that the reflective nature of the journal was the illuminating torch toward his self-revelation. But, in reality, I have no clear answer. Teaching can be an inexact science.

Perhaps Marvin heard a call in his journal—a call to action, a call to rise to the challenge, a call to find the meaning that is within all of us. Perhaps, we as teachers are there to guide students to find that call. And, in the process, if we're lucky, we hear it, too. I did, and it has made all of the difference.

Brandy Price has been a teacher since she was eight—first holding neighborhood kids captive in a makeshift classroom before moving on to a more formal setting. She earned her teaching credential at U.C.L.A. and went on to teach nearly every level from kindergarten through post-secondary. In 2003, she earned National Board Certification. She is currently the principal of Ingenium Charter School in Canoga Park, California. Her professional goal is for Ingenium to become a California Distinguished School by its third year of operations. Brandy's favorite book as a child was *The Little Engine That Could*, an inspirational tale that she believes unfolds again and again every single day in schools across the country.

Articulating the Blur

Laurie Zum Hofe

"My sense is that the American character lives not in one place or the other but in the gaps between the places ,and in our struggles to be together in our differences. It lives not in what has been fully articulated but in what is in the process of being articulated, not in the smooth-sounding words but in the very moment that the smooth sounding words fail us."[2]

There is a palpable disparity between those few feet, easily crossed with a few steps in a few seconds. Usually, on one side, there is bustling exuberance, loud conversation, chaotic movement navigated with little direction. On the other, there is seated silence, prompted questions, little movement assigned with much direction. Seemingly, there is an invisible boundary drawn between the hallway and the classroom that further complicates and blurs the boundary between life and school. When students and teachers move through that gap with a step through a classroom doorway, a transformation occurs. Who we are on one side is not always who we are on the other side.

What happens when that boundary is either forcibly or voluntarily crossed, when the hallway of life seeps into the classroom of school? I used to think blurred boundaries meant problems to avoid. I shied away from sharing too much about my personal experiences. "I shouldn't want the students to know too much about who I am outside of the classroom," I told myself. I approached my students' emotional stories with much caution. "I shouldn't look vulnerable in front of them," I argued to myself.

But vulnerability and emotion aren't just vague ideas we analyze in the stories we read; they are clearly present on faces and in gestures and between lines, read and written and spoken. When classrooms become spaces alive with stories and people who have lived them in their hardness, their grace and their beauty, these moments of reality that sneak over the classroom threshold, while discomforting and uneasy, can provoke possibilities to learn.

Here's how it all started to get blurry.

Articulation Attempt 1: Monday, Introduction to Literature class

Today, my college students and I are discussing Cormac McCarthy's *The Road*, a narrative about a post-apocalyptic world where a father and son journey down the road together. McCarthy's narrative uses little punctuation, especially with quotations around dialogue. Conversation between father and son is simplistic and sparse. The majority of my students have been resistant to the text.

"What is the point of the book?" they ask-argue.

I am hesitant to tell them that I devoured the book myself, mostly curious, if not obsessed, about finding out what actually happened to the world. I find myself strangely unsatisfied at the book's conclusion, but my teacherly self is intrigued. McCarthy himself never answers that question, instead focusing solely on the father-son relationship. After spending more time than I had planned on this "I hated this book" discussion this Monday afternoon, I feel the pressure of the clock to move on. But students cycle around each other's verbal thoughts, trying to come to some sense about the "meaning" behind the book.

"What about the book has you so dissatisfied?" I ask the group. Philip goes out on a limb. He rarely contributes unless moved by the spirit of something.

"The whole thing, the ending, the plot, the story. It just had no point," he huffs.

David replies, "But maybe that's the point. Maybe it wasn't about anything but the father and son on the road. Maybe the lines of dialogue and the grey description of everything symbolize the world they live in now, the desolation."

Kelsey raises her hand. I keep telling this class that raising of hands is not necessary, but they resist it, keeping the classroom boundaries in place. I nod to her. "I just hated this book," she begins. "I don't understand why someone would write a book that has no meaning to it. I just can't put into words what I feel. I'm just frustrated." In her response to *1984*, Kelsey also wrote about her frustrations throughout her reading of that book. I encouraged her to keep seeking out questions, trying to find helpful ways of naming that frustration. I remind her of *1984* now.

"You said some similar things about *1984*, Kelsey. I'm still interested in why you think this frustration is going on," I smile.

"I don't know why," Kelsey admits. "And it's really bothering me."

I turn to the entire class and say, "This resistance is something I think that we all should keep attending to. Why is it that we are so unsatisfied? What makes our sense-making frustrating?"

Philip more emphatically participates, "Because the plot wasn't like the chart I'm used to. There wasn't a climax and then the line that goes down fast." As I imagine the arrows and the boxes with rising action and falling action, I hear what I might poetically call a chorus of "amens" from the rest of the class. "Yeah," says Philip, charged with the approval of the chorus, "the plot was just a flat-line." Nods. "Uhm-hmms" echo around the room.

I move from the front of the room where I've been standing and writing on the board, nonverbally directing my control of the classroom. Instead, I sit on a desk top, moving closer to my students' levels, blurring my stance of authority. "So here's my question," I say. "Is life like the plot development chart? Can we chart the climaxes and the dénouements of our lives?" I immediately see Dustin shake his head and make eye contact with me. This semester, Dustin is dealing with the recent and unexpected death of his father. He's been emailing apologies for missing class. He wants me to know that he's having a rough time and he'll do whatever he needs to do to pass the class. But he isn't sleeping and struggles for relief from his grief. I want this book to be relief to Dustin, to recognize himself in the father-son relationship, that the son continues on because of the father. But I don't know if that blurs boundaries too much. Is it my job to offer him relief?

David speaks up again, "We're frustrated because of the flatline and the elusive meaning."

Other students chime in. "Because we can't figure out what it means."

"Where does that come from?" I ask.

Another student smirks from the back row. "From years and years of English teachers," he says. "Here's how I see it," he continues. "If I can't find enjoyment in a book, then it just doesn't matter to me. I have to find some connection to my life, or the book is worthless to me." I want to ask him if enjoyment and connection to his life are synonymous, but another student interrupts before I have the chance.

"I don't know if I would go so far as to say that I need to enjoy the book because in a way I did want to keep reading it to find out what happened, but I still don't know what it means," she says. Students murmur agreement and the clock winds down. I sigh. Why do I feel the need to have closure on something I know shouldn't have to be "closed?" I feel guilty and unsatisfied, eager to return to clear boundaries, and I leave my seat on the desktop amidst the students and stand up in the front where I safely belong. I move to end class for the day.

Articulation Attempt 2: Monday, After Class

Students get up and make their way eagerly to the door and then the hallway. Kelsey lingers and then approaches.

She pauses and then speaks, "So I know you're not supposed to write notes during class, but I wrote one to you." She hands me a folded up piece of lined notebook paper, with "Proffessor Z." on it, the second "f" crossed out in blue pen.

I say "thanks." When safe in my office, I sigh and I read:

I was going to email this to you but I didn't want to forget so I just thought I'd write it now in class. (I kind of feel like I'm being bad cause I'm writing notes in class but since I'm writing to you I guess it's OK) I think the reason the Road put me into that weird mood was because it made me feel a little bit selfish and I realized that I take a lot for granted. There are people out there who are homeless and cold and have no family but I'm here at a very expensive college and I have all I need and all the love I could ask for but I complain about stupid little things. Also I think it gave me a reality check. I love to look at the world through rose-colored glasses but this book kind of gave me a slap in the face. I just always thought that if I was homeless I would be able to survive and work my way back up but this book basically said there was no hope and there is a lot of evil in the world too and I don't like to think about the bad stuff in the world which is probably a bad idea because it kind of makes me nieve (I don't know how to spell it) and ignorant but I just don't think I'm ready to grow up yet. So that's my feelings and I realize this note is very scatterbrained but I was trying to pay attention to class and I wasn't exactly sure what I was feeling yet either so I just wrote it down what came to mind and it didn't come out clearly. Sorry. Also, I wanted to say thanks for pushing me to go the extra mile instead of stopping short (you kind of remind me of my cross country coach). So thank you for getting me into this class.

I lean back in my chair. I sigh again. Someone comfortable with a clear classroom boundary might imagine herself a hero. But, once it starts to get blurry, it's too easy a move to make. I don't see how hero worship helps me learn, and I feel like I need to learn what to do here. That there should be some book that makes this blurriness easier and less unsettling. What do I do next? I feel as if my next step is essential, crucial and necessary in some big way, but I don't know how to think about the bigness. And I'm supposed to be the teacher, the one who stands knowing and certain. Am I too much like my students? Are my questions about the elusive right answer? I kind of feel like there is a right answer and a wrong answer here, and the blur dissipates in the light of safety and certainty. I find myself wishing the blur back. I lean into my questions. I open up a new email document and write to Kelsey.

Articulation Attempt #3: Emailing with Kelsey

Kelsey,
Never in my life have I been so nicely compared to someone in the athletic field, so thanks for that. And also, thanks for pushing me to be the kind of instructor that keeps asking questions. I really enjoy your presence and your resistance and I'm happy that you felt so moved to write this response in class. You're moving in a hard direction, the direction that recognizes that the world is not completely a place that loves and tries to seek the good. It's a hard, hard place at times. And here, where we are, it's hard to remember that; in fact, it's easy to be resistant to it. But I applaud your efforts to keep working in that direction. And I want to know what you think we should do about it.

I think it's one thing to say "I'm having these realizations" and another to do something about those realizations. How can we be do-ers, Kelsey? And I mean that outside of our college dwelling and outside of the English classes. What will we do with what the literature awakens in us? Good/Bad/In between/On the Road?

I use "we" purposely here, because I feel the urge to do, but I don't quite know what to do with the urge. Does that make sense? Let's keep talking about this one.

I'm proud of you for walking alongside the resistance instead of just leaving it behind.

Professor Z.

Kelsey's response:

In high school I went and worked at a soup kitchen a couple of times. It was in a pretty rough town but I stopped going 'cause I did sports and I always had homework or something else to do. Now that I think about it, though, that's one of the things that The Road made me think about. I should've gone more often. I really could've made the time for it but I went to the basketball games instead and hung out with friends. Maybe we should go to a soup kitchen as a class or something. I don't know if that's what you were looking for but I'm just throwing out ideas. Also, I keep forgetting to e-mail you about that 1984 paper. I've left myself about 100 sticky notes on my desk but I just keep forgetting. Could I possibly just come to your office one day and talk about it? I do a lot better when I can talk about things instead of writing them cause I like to use my hands and its easier for me to have a conversation about it. Also, I've kind of started to forget some parts of the book and why I was so frustrated so a discussion might be easier. If you don't like that idea, though, I can understand because I can see where you'd want me to get better at putting my feelings down on paper. Just let me know what you think.

Thanks,
Kelsey

Articulation Attempt #4: Tuesday: Planning for Wednesday's Class

"'Only when the boundary is recognized as moveable can it be a regenerative element in art, rather than an obstacle to its growth.'"[3]

A day later, I still can't get the conversation, verbal and written, with Kelsey out of my mind. Something is moving and at work in the glances we share, between the lines of our shared and dissonant ideas. I'm supposed to be the teacher with some big, life-changing answer, to respond with this felt, underlying critical pedagogical sense and I got nothin'. I wrote back to Kelsey's above email that we should keep talking about it together, but I feel today like it's a copout.

My copping out is also rooted in those clear, traditional, expected boundaries in which we have been schooled. I see my students looking for correct interpretations, aiming to please the teacher, to get the A, to complete the course, to get the credit.

And then I get a quickly scribbled note from Kelsey and underlying my excitement, my awareness of boundary, I'm scared. What do I do with this all-important moment? Towards what could it lead? Away from what safe boundaries could we travel?

I see Kelsey frustrated, and part of me wants to know how to keep that frustration moving and part of me wants to find the elusive meaning of *The Road*, too. I want to awkwardly giggle at Kelsey's solution of the soup kitchen, and, at the same time, I want to hug her for thinking of it as a possibility. I want to keep my pencil moving, to keep tapping at the keys of my computer to reach that elusive something. Is that what this blur is: an obstacle that frustrates but intrigues at the same time?

Articulation Attempt #5: Wednesday's Class

Today's date is the day I dread most in the year. It's the anniversary of the day my mom died, and, while much time has passed since then, the day never gets easier. I just get more used to it. In class today, I look at Dustin and see myself there, in his hunched over upper body, with his cap on, hood up, in his nodding about the complications of plot (life) development.

I always feel a little "off" during this day, and today is no exception. I always wonder how to dwell in the classroom and deal with the weight of my memories in the same space. Today there's a part of me that wants to reveal my story, wants to share with my students that if it hasn't happened already, it will. Life will hit and the rose-colored glasses will come off. But that would be a blurry lecture and one most likely rooted in grief, one learned in pain and in life, not from a teacher or in a classroom. I look around this classroom, and I see another student who lost her dad last March. In her hand movements today, disagreeing with her classmates, I see the grief move.

I look at Dustin as we talk about the complex vocabulary of *Ella Minnow Pea*, our next text. I see him look back.

"I'm a simple man," he says, prompted perhaps by my glance. "Give me an 'a,' a 'the,' I'm happy." I know that Dustin longs for simplicity again. And then another student disagrees with everyone and uses words like "correct answer" and "it's not right unless..." and I feel the students long for clarity of answer, leaning away from the complicated and messy. I wonder how we have led them to this, taught them that easy and correct is best.

In some way, I want to say that there will be a time when correct answers will be elusive, that what was "right" will never be "right" again. And I want to bring that complication and complexity of life into my classroom. But words are elusive to me on this day. I long to put up the boundary of my non-existent hood and simplify, hunch over and just get through the class. It's hard to have any kind of answers when you're reminded of difference, conflict, and interruption in a way that academic plot charts can never predict. And the questions for me remain in a real way today, their presence a heavy burden. Some days, it feels too risky to move to the blur, to make the attempt to articulate. Some days, after class, much like my students, I long for "easy" and "correct" as I walk out of the classroom, moving those few steps into the hallway and into my life.

Laurie Zum Hofe received a B.S. in education from Concordia University (Nebraska) and an M.A. in writing from DePaul University in Chicago. She is an assistant professor of English at her alma mater, Concordia University, in Seward, Nebraska, where she teaches writing, literature, and pre-service English education courses. A former elementary and middle school teacher in Minnesota and Illinois, she is currently a doctoral candidate at the University of Nebraska-Lincoln, studying the use of emotion in composition classrooms. Education runs in her blood; she is among the fifth generation of teachers in her family.

The Myth of the Teacher

Kurt Reynolds

On rainy summer days, my grandmother used to snatch a title from her bookcase, sit down in her recliner, nestle me in her lap, and open new worlds to me. It only took a few lines before I forget about the dark skies outside while she read *Watership Down*, *Huckleberry Finn*, *The Hobbit*, and *Grimm's Fairy Tales*. Of all the stories she read, though, one has stayed with me: the myth of Sisyphus from Edith Hamilton's *Mythology*. His eternal punishment was almost too much for my seven-year-old mind the first time Granny recounted his tale. Sisyphus is cursed to lug a boulder up a steep mountain, only to deliver it to the top and have it plummet back to the bottom. For all of his labor, he is forever toiling in futility.

Even the eternal lake of fire the nuns frightened us with at catechism didn't horrify me the way Sisyphus' fate did. I couldn't imagine a punishment worse than to work so hard, only to suffer failure after failure . . . for all eternity.

As a high school English teacher, I am well acquainted with his plight. Don't get me wrong, there are dozens of moments every class period where I experience moments of great success. There is the satisfied smile on a student's face when she opens up her research paper and sees the "A" scrawled across the top. There is the wide-eyed shock on several students' faces when they reach the conclusion of Shirley Jackson's "The Lottery" and realize what it means for the winner. There is the debate that erupts in class over a podcast featuring Mark Bauerlein, author of *The Dumbest Generation*, when the class realizes the author's title is referring to *their* generation. These moments are sublime; they keep me in this profession. Despite these moments, though, I know that I will ultimately fail in some way with every one of my students. I am a real life version of Sisyphus.

I squat, dig my heels in, place my shoulder against the granite, and with all my strength from my toes to my neck, I push. The boulder budges an inch. I don't dare a look up the mountain. I keep my eyes focused on the ground and being my ascent...

That is how I feel when I begin a class. I am eager to do the work, to see my students learn. I am focused on one goal: engaging my students in the learning process. Yet, as students flood in with iPod buds burrowed in their ears, Blackberries clenched in their fists, and talk of last night's hockey game on their tongues, I know the mountain is steep.

The rock is smooth against my face, minute particles of dirt grind between my clinching teeth, and drops of sweat sprout on my forehead and forearms as I inch up the mountain . . .

Surely, a single school year is not eternity. But multiply 169 student days by the 30 kids in each of my three classes, and I have at least 15,210 trips up that mountain.

I have the boulder half way up the mountain. The footing is more treacherous. The rock seems twice as heavy up here . . . Most of my students turn in their responses to last night's reading assignment. There are two, though, who have nothing to turn in. It has been that way for weeks. There are several who begin to concoct excuses, "I had to work until eleven" and "I emailed it to you! What do you mean you didn't get it?" and "Our printer was out of ink." Despite this, I push on . . .

The knowledge that I want to engage my students with is my boulder. Somewhere along the journey, the rock inevitably slips and careens back to the bottom. This occurs in a number of ways. First, a student can simply refuse to partake in my class. Mark peers out the window and watches the elementary kids play football across the street. He texts his girlfriend from the cell phone crammed in the front pocket of his jeans. Second, I can fail to make a student understand. Jacob isn't able to penetrate Shakespeare's prose, no matter how many vocabulary worksheets we do, how many times we read the footnotes, or how many times we translate the text into modern English. Third, I may engage a student and get them to grasp a key concept, but do all my students make the connection? I know Bryce understands the irony in the title of Tim O'Brien's Vietnam war story, "The Things They Carried," because his older brother fought in Iraq and now has his own burden of memories with which to deal. But do others relate to it? Fourth, a student may get the main idea of the lesson yet struggle putting it all together. They get frustrated and shut down. Jena can write a thesis statement, but she can't get her supporting paragraphs to fit in with her thesis. There are countless ways a teacher fails every single period, every single day.

I am almost at the crest. Sheer gravity has made the boulder and me nearly one . . . I have most of the class engaged. They are discussing the documentary I showed based on last night's reading. Time flies. Then we realize there are ten minutes left in class. Some students keep discussing while others shut down. They clear their books off their desks and shuffle them into their backpacks. Cell phones appear on desks. Several turn and visit with those behind them. One even dares to meander to the door, ready to be the first one free. Seeking a moment of relief, I dare sigh. The ground so stable on my ascent, suddenly gives . . .

***

Last Memorial weekend, I was cleaning my room and found an old textbook, *Themes in World Literature*.[4] I couldn't help but page through it, scanning the authors and titles. An essay entitled "The Myth of Sisyphus" by Albert Camus seized my attention. It changed my view of Sisyphus forever.

Camus casts Sisyphus not as a wretch toiling forever in futility; rather, Camus casts him as a hero, arguing that while Sisyphus's struggle seems to be in vain, it is really just the opposite. While it is true every effort to deliver the rock to the crest of that mountain is met with disappointment, it is also true that when the boulder inevitably tumbles back to the bottom, Sisyphus has time to reflect on his return. It is on his return that Sisyphus becomes heroic. Here he is aware of his fate. He does not toil in vain; Sisyphus is conscious of his fate. It is his fate, of his doing. Thus, he is master of it.

Camus reasons that since Sisyphus is conscious of his fate (he has no illusions about ever getting his boulder over the crest) he can take pleasure in the work, as Camus writes, "All Sisyphus's silent joy is constrained therein. His fate belongs to him. His rock is his thing" (231). Is it tragic? Certainly. But it is his consciousness that makes it tragic and, at the same time, heroic.

The boulder rushes back down. I sigh, aching from head to toe. I take a deep breath, look out over the top of the mountain. I exhale, letting the breath go free and descend . . . grinning.

I may never push the rock over the top. Despite this, I also become master of my fate. I now can enjoy the work, hopeless as it may be. I can revel in the toil. I can rejoice in my effort. For it is a worthy effort. Teaching is noble. It is attempting the impossible. I know I will never teach every single student every single day every single thing I intend. What is important is the work. The task. The exalted effort. As Camus concludes, "The struggle itself toward the heights is enough to fill a man's heart. One must imagine Sisyphus happy" (232). My fate belongs to me. My teaching is my thing. It is tragic, but above all, heroic.

I squat, dig my heels in, place my shoulder against the granite, and with all my strength from my toes to my neck, I push. The boulder budges an inch. I don't dare a look up the mountain. I keep my eyes focused on the ground, charting my progress inch by inch . . .

Kurt Reynolds attended Bemidji State University in Minnesota where he earned his M.A. in English and a B.S. in English education. Recently, he completed a master's program in Minnesota history through Hamline University. For the past fourteen years, he has taught high school English at Lincoln High School in Thief River Falls, Minnesota. He is currently teaching College in the High School classes, presents demonstrations to teachers, staff, and administrators in Minnesota and North Dakota on using technology in the English classroom, and serves as a teaching consultant with the Red River Valley Writing Project through the University of North Dakota. He lives with his wife and four children in Thief River Falls. You can follow him on twitter via @teacherscribe or visit his blog: *www.teacherscribe.blogspot.com.*

Not Just Funny Stories

Alanna Navitski

At the bar down the street from my old school, we used to get free drinks when we showed off our bite marks from work. We used to get free drinks a lot. That's because I worked at a pre-school for young children with special needs, including autism, emotional disturbances, behavioral issues, speech and language delays...a laundry list of struggles and sparks of peculiar brilliance. Those kids were small but endlessly creative in their attempts to escape, avoid, provoke, and communicate their needs in somewhat confusing, but very honest, ways. In my students' attempts to get their points across, I also lost some chunks of hair, got drenched by a hose wielded with maniacal laughter, and carried an seventy-pound four year old for half a mile. I participated in many dramatic chase scenes in pursuit of preschoolers on the lam...down the block, through the park, over and under the tables. Not to mention my many interesting experiences with some of the less appealing bodily functions. It didn't take long to get over any surprise at ending up with pee on my lap or being thrown up on, but even my jaded self was somewhat surprised when a child began peeing in a bucket in the middle of the classroom, and by a later incident involving pee raining through the fence edging our Brooklyn roof-top playground onto the street below. And I never did quite figure out quite what was going on with the little balls of poop that I used to find hidden stealthily around the classroom after naptime.

These are good stories, and they would likely be amusing cocktail party anecdotes, if I do say so myself. But that's not why I still do my job. And it's not because of the free drinks, either. I also don't do it for the twenty or so dollars an hour I make (less if you count all the planning time), and I don't do it for the cooing that happens at the aforementioned cocktail parties when I tell people what I do, the sigh of, "Oh, you must be so patient," accompanied by a certain softening of the eyes that is usually reserved for cute videos of kittens on YouTube.

I do it because there aren't many other jobs that involve engaging with the big questions and struggles of life on a daily basis, that allow for such a clear view of so many of the profound aspects of being human on this planet. There aren't many jobs that require such deep respect for people and that offer such evidence of treasures in return.

So what does teaching mean? Teaching means listening really hard and watching and waiting. It means believing that each of your students has something important to show you, if you can look from just the right angle to catch the glint of the gem. It means rejoicing in the endless variation of ways of thinking, ways of knowing, ways of creating. It means working really hard to understand each of your students as a full and complex person because only through knowing where students are can teachers move them to the next step. It means trying really hard to send your reluctant ego on a weekend getaway, so you can see another person clearly, so you can listen to another's voice without the interference of your own prejudgment.

Teaching means that you are an optimist. It means that, despite so much evidence to the contrary, there is a part of you that believes that the world is a big and beautiful place that is worth knowing about. It means that you believe that people can change, that things do not have to be the way that they are, that with some hard work and some careful planning, miracles can happen. And the amazing thing about teaching is that, sometimes, they actually do. Lots of times they don't, and it breaks your heart every time. But sometimes they do, and you get to have the thrilling knowledge that you helped to make them happen.

Teaching means that you show up…every single day. It means that even if that morning, for some reason, the glass lid of the pasta pot arbitrarily exploded all over the kitchen and then the handle broke off the coffee pot spilling hot coffee all over your chest that is only partly covered by a ripped tank top because it's six in the morning, and then the subway stalled, so you couldn't get coffee on the way to school because you were late. Even if all of that happened (and it did), when you show up, you do not go into your office and shut the door until you get to drink some coffee. You do not yell at those less powerful than you and tell them to bring you coffee. You do not stare mindlessly at your computer and post on Facebook about what a bad morning you had and how much you want coffee. Instead, you go into your classroom, and you do what you have to do. Teaching means that you put your needs to the side because someone else is more important. If you try to do that all the time, you may die or be very cranky and bitter. But, for that part of the day when you are standing in front of students, that's what you do, and you get through it. Maybe you are snappy, and the kids stare at you and wonder where their nice teacher went, but you are there, and you don't smash anything or throw the annoying kid out the window. You are dependable, and you are trustworthy, and you endure. No matter what. Teaching means demonstrating what it means to be steady, and to make it through, to show that life is hard, but we survive despite it all.

Along with that drudgery comes persistence. Teaching means working really hard at something, maybe at planning your lesson and getting it wrong. And then trying it again and getting it wrong again and then thinking about it when you are at the beach and when you are eating breakfast and when you are taking your cat to the vet, and dreaming about it, and then trying it again and again until you get it right. Because what you are trying to do is important. It means that you watch other people do the same, watch them make mistakes and try and fail, and fail again, and then you help them figure out a way to try it again anyway. Teaching means that you watch struggle and heartbreak and things that are just too hard, and you hold it all in your hands, and you don't go away.

I've never been one to refuse free drinks, and having access to some cocktail party capital isn't so bad, either. But I could live without all of those things, and still find joy and pride in my work because of the deep way in which I get to know my students, because of the way that we meet challenges and survive together, because of the miracles that happen every once in a while. Despite outside pressures, I can still see my students as people, none of them quite the same. I know what teaching means. But I'm not sure that many policy-makers do. I am working on figuring out how to teach them and crossing my fingers that they will learn.

Alanna Navitski is an early interventionist and teacher educator. Alanna's students range from toddler-hood to adulthood. This allows her to witness the learning process of a wide variety of unique, amazing, and crazy-making people. She worked for several years in a therapeutic nursery school for children with special needs and inclusive preschools in New York City and assisted in running an early intervention program for families. Currently, she is a fieldwork advisor and course instructor at Bank Street College in New York City and also continues to work with young children. In all settings, Alanna has sought to create learning communities in which all members feel competent, express their ideas confidently, and listen hard to one another. When she is not busy washing finger paint out of her professor clothes, Alanna is active in community organizing for social justice in education and works on projects with the New York Collective of Radical Educators and other New York City groups.

Ten Reasons Why I'm Not Going to Quit Teaching and Become a Full-Time Chicken Farmer...This Year

Cathy Walker-Gilman

There seem to be some strange misconceptions floating around about public school teachers these days. Having been in this field for the past seventeen years, since the day I completed my licensure program, I am somewhat perplexed by the gross generalizations and negativity oozing into my classroom. You know how sometimes a politically motivated organization will draw attention to a non-existent problem in order to draw attention away from a real one? I'm just saying.

Don't get me wrong. I absolutely believe that there are problems with the current public education system. But I also believe that it is the largest amalgamation of dedicated, enthusiastic, creative individuals to be found on this planet. It would be refreshing for the inhabitants of the "real world" to head into the classrooms of those of us who believe in what we do in order to experience the reality of being an educator in the United States in 2011.

Primarily, I am a teacher of writing. I also care for four chickens in our urban backyard. We get fresh eggs every day, killer compost, and an education in sustainability and responsibility. There have been days in the past year where I have considered the benefits of quitting my job, donning dungarees and Wellington boots, and scooping poop all day long. Then I remember the mortgage, and daycare, and swim class, and groceries, and my dream deflates. But there you have it. My husband is a teacher, too. Unless one of us transforms into a lawyer or a doctor or a Trump, we both have to work to support our family. So I've spent some time here trying to justify my existence, to rationalize the work of the public school teacher, and to find hope in a hostile environment. This is my manifesto. Brace yourself.

1. I have the energy to help any child grow as a writer.

Nothing gives me more hope or inspiration than watching a child's eyes light up and knowing that they are about to take a chance, to explore unknown territory, to write with abandon. We write together. We write a lot. We write because it makes us strong. I can write all day long, and the kids need to see this. They need to see the messes, the successes, the revisions, and the possibilities evolve in front of them before they feel entitled to join the fun. I am privileged to be the ringmaster at this nutty middle school circus.

2. I have the opportunity to teach children the power of words.

Some days, I am a super hero. I can reinvent words, defy the rules of syntax, manipulate grammar, and make a ruckus with a pen and a spiral notebook. You bet I can. Even with standardized Kryptonite glowing menacingly in the distance. And the more fun I have with my ego in this marvelous spiral of composition, the more my children hear my voice. The more they hear my voice, the more they talk to me in their own voices. Once they admit that they each have a unique voice, they naturally exercise their right to use them to take a stand, defend an argument, change the world. Cape not included.

3. I have the desire to engage children with new and exciting technology.

When I learn about a new application or website that might make language more accessible, and dare I say, fun, for children, I share it. I consume it. When I don't understand it, I ask questions. Lots of questions. Sometimes the children can help me learn, sometimes I can lead them to a new place. Either way, I view technology as my ally and I integrate it with enthusiasm so my children will have a fighting chance to excel in the real world. If I can't get the "doc camera" to work until a student points out that I have failed to plug it in, so be it. I am happy to be the dunce in the name of progress. Just don't make me stand in the corner.

4. I have the strength to hear children's secrets without judgment.

When children find their voices, they speak their minds. Sometimes, well truthfully, most times this leads to some drama and trauma. And that is a double-edged sword. How privileged am I to work in a context where honesty and confession are not precursors to guilt? But then there are days when I wish I could erase the words on the page I've just read, reimagine reality for a child in crisis. There are moments when it hurts to be a teacher. But when a child invites me into a sacred space on the page, I have a window of opportunity to make a difference, to listen, to act. Every child deserves to be heard, and I am a pretty good listener.

5. I have the tenacity to give every child one more chance.

When a child turns in an essay written in green crayon, or farts just to see who will be the most offended, sharpens a pencil in the middle of a guest speaker's presentation, "forgets" to turn in homework for the 17th time, I get a little frazzled. It's only fair. How would people in the "real world" react when faced with similar scenarios? An interesting question. But I take a deep breath (except in the case of the fart) and release it slowly. I close my eyes. And then I resume as if nothing has happened. Because the education of all 113 of my students is far more weighty a consideration than faltering in the face of rigidity. Wouldn't you allow your own children to learn from their mistakes? Even the smelly ones? That's what I thought.

6. I have the optimism to believe that things can only

improve.

These are dark times for teachers. I believe I am good at my job, that I am good for my students, but still I feel I am under attack. Seriously, at what other juncture beyond the years of public education are people in this country expected to produce flawless work without benefit of peer and mentor collaboration, and a plethora of tools and technologies? Never, that's when. So I have the naiveté to believe that somewhere down the road light will dawn and the disconnect between fantasy and reality will emerge for public consideration. I maintain that most of us have the greater good in mind. We don't come to work every day to fill innocent children's heads with poison and despair. Not on most days, at least. So I resolve to see the coffee carafe as half full of fair-traded, shade grown, Colombian goodness rather than empty and stained with generic, day-old grounds.

7. I have the flexibility to embrace change.

It would be easy to present the same canned curriculum every year, read the same books, give the same tests. But my kids are not clones. They do not fall off an assembly line into my classroom and sit passively in their desks. Sometimes they sit under them. Because of the varied backgrounds and beliefs of my students, I am compelled to constantly reconfigure and evaluate what I do every day in the classroom. If something works in second period, it may well crash and burn during fifth. There is no consistency, no logic to the way children learn. By default, I have to be willing to drink the Kool-Aid from time to time, to take a chance on a new direction or an unusual idea. What is happening in public education right now works for some kids, but not all. The missing piece that escapes public attention is that there is no single methodology, textbook, or consequence that will cause every child to respond. It is my responsibility to punt when necessary, and keep my eyes open.

8. I have the humility to learn from my own mistakes.

I may be a super hero, but I'm definitely not perfect. There are days when I am not 100% focused on the growth of my students. I admit this freely. But these days are few, and I smack myself upside the head and regroup pretty efficiently when I realize I'm in a slump. Because with up to 30 voices clamoring in your general direction at any given time, teachers can't afford to be slackers for more than a split second without being eaten alive. But sometimes I'm cranky, and it impacts the way I engage with writers and writing. Sometimes I lose faith, which causes me to lose momentum. Sometimes I say the wrong thing, and I pay the price. But it's hard to stay silent when most children are being left behind in one way or another. When (not if) I stick my foot in my mouth I admit my error, rant, then make nice. Everybody screws up; it's even acceptable for children to see this happen to adults. What is not acceptable is to blame the children for the missteps of the grown-ups in their lives. When students apologize to me for moments of dubious judgment, I tell them not to say sorry, but to change their behavior. Common sense.

9. I have the passion to change the world.

I may have impacted a few lives over the past 17 years, from taking Sylvia home every day after summer school to buying Anthony a book of poetry at the end of the year. You know, the little things. But I'd like to think that Sylvia and Anthony went out of their way at some juncture to perpetuate an understanding of human decency because they witnessed it being modeled one day. This is not about feeding some twisted sort of narcissism; that wasn't listed anywhere in the job description. Most teachers I know, if you take the time to ask them, will tell you that the reason they got into teaching was to make a difference in children's lives. Does that sound corny? I guess it probably does. But it's true. Children are sponges; we all know that. They absorb the energy that surrounds them, positive or negative, and decide whether to emulate it or reject it. So I choose to model compassion, diversity, and joy.

10. I have the courage to voice my beliefs and act on them.

If a child is being marginalized within about a ten mile radius, I feel it is my duty as a caretaker, as a global citizen, as a parent, to embrace the difference that relegates that individual to the fringe, and celebrate it. If I am told that I cannot be honest with my students, I will not comply. If I am told I cannot laugh with them, I'll turn my back. We will write and talk about topics that are taboo, and we will explore new worlds together. I will defend the rights of my students, my colleagues, and myself to freely discuss multiple perspectives. And we will all grow stronger as a result of these conversations. At the times when my students feel they have no voice, I will help them to find one. And I will stand with them and speak with them and show them the power of eloquence.

Chickens will be chickens, and children will be children, and chumps will be chumps. Between these three options, I choose the company of the children. I grow moment by moment because of my interactions with my students. It is my privilege to be a part of their world. The fowl will have to ride in the backseat for the time-being. Metaphorically, of course. Because at the end of the day, I am a public school teacher, and I am proud of the work I do.

❖ ❖ ❖

Cathy Walker-Gilman is a sixth grade language arts teacher at Campus Middle School in Greenwood Village, Colorado. She is a fellow of the Colorado Writing Project and the Denver Writing Project. She has been writing since she could hold a crayon; these days she tends to word-process. Cathy has self-published a book of short stories, *Margin Notes*, about young adults surviving on the fringes. She is working on a young adult novel about a homeless gourmand and has plans for two other tomes percolating in her addled brain. Cathy lives with her husband, two children, two cats, and four chickens on a bit of an urban homestead in Denver.

Teaching Means Standing Up and Speaking Out

Santo

Karl Meiner

One of our college students was shot dead in late May. He was affiliated with a G.E.D. program that feeds into one of our Early College Programs. From all accounts, he was ebullient, hard working, and eager to forge a path to a brighter future. He was also Latino; his family had immigrated to Oregon from Mexico. In the end, the media chose to use that fact to stoke the narrow-minded flames of bigotry which continue to suppress many of our nation's youth. Santo was the student of one of my colleagues. I didn't know him. But many of the young adults I teach as a writing instructor at a branch of Chemeketa Community College did know him.

He was, in so many respects, representative of most of them. At nineteen, he had relatives who had crossed the border in the dark of night to reach the promised land. At nineteen, he had relatives who spent countless hours in the field picking fruit. At nineteen, he saw beyond the small Oregon town he lived in and dreamt of a college degree. At nineteen, he was shot to death on his front porch in a case of mistaken identity. But to the media that covered the shooting, he was another just Latino gang banger who fell victim to the violence that he begat. Santo was never part of a gang.

Most of my students at the Woodburn branch of Chemeketa are the first generation in their families to matriculate from the U.S. public school system. They write about how their parents crossed from Arizona or California and migrated north to the heavily Mexican community here with the classic dreams of providing more for their families. These are sharp, motivated young adults. But, for most of them, English is a second language.

When they arrive in my introductory, college writing classes, my assignment is to open the language to them. In a sense, I work to demystify the rules of grammar and make them accessible. Their bright, youthful eyes shine in stark contrast to the dark circles that accentuate them. As they dutifully take notes on punctuation and

M.L.A. formatting, they mentally prepare themselves for the full-time jobs that await them after school. I lose several each term because they have to support their families. Many work in the fields, for instance, awaking long before sunrise to pick the fruit, which is sold at upscale supermarkets in Portland. They often take time off because of a work-related injury either to themselves or, often, one of their parents. In every respect, they are some of the hardest working people I have ever known in my life. And, in every waking moment, they work tirelessly to dispel the cultural misconceptions, which seek to define them.

I am fortunate to work in a program, which, at its core, embodies the finest values of the American educational system. We take students who have finished their high school education and provide them with further academic skills necessary for college success. As our nation's economy was rendered impotent by rapacious investment firms playing roulette with the middle class, I was engaged with second language students who could deconstruct the function of every word in a compound-complex sentence. My students come to me hungry: they are starving for meaningful, lasting employment and for an education that isn't hidden behind tens of thousands of dollars they neither possess nor can borrow.

And as each Oregon spring winds to a moist close, I would wager that these eager young minds could elucidate far more precisely than most of our politicians about the proper way to compose a meaningful essay. They could also teach them a thing or two about altruism and dedication. But to so many, they are just Mexican-American kids draining the public coffers. I wish they could see what I see.

When the news decided to cover Santo's tragic death, it was framed as gang-related. This was no doubt a reflex reaction to his heritage. The students who knew him emphatically refuted this stereotype. Santo, they said, was a good kid. Santo's death at the hand of another young person was a horrifically tragic case of mistaken identity. What the news won't discuss is that the larger, systemic tragedy is how politics, the media, and pundits are misdirecting economic fears onto our nation's most promising young adults. Our nation is simultaneously casting the shadow of the "other" upon immigrants and their children while vilifying the educational system as public waste. We are taught to study the news out of fear. We are trained to find someone to project this fear onto. My students are an easy target. The result, ultimately, is that we perpetuate an ugly pattern of alienating some of our most ambitious students. They are left as two-dimensional caricatures which serve as shallow talking points about immigration reform for puffy candidates seeking votes at their expense. The tragedy is that our entire populace is deprived of potential. There are future doctors, engineers, teachers, and artists whose potential is being extinguished for political gamesmanship.

I am proud to work as an educator for this population. Every time I read that some regional politician is seeking to build their name by denigrating Mexican immigrants or the pension plans of public employees, I need only to think about how tirelessly my students work in and out of my classroom. If the academic skills that I pass on to them give them any advantage as they craft their futures, I have hope that, as a nation, we'll devote ourselves to supporting, and not alienating, youth like Santo. He deserves that sort of legacy.

Karl Meiner earned his B.A. in English literature from the University of Arizona and went on to complete an M.A. from Portland State University and then an M.A.T. from Lewis and Clark College. Karl teaches college writing at Chemeketa Community College on both its Salem and Woodburn campuses. He has lived in Portland, Oregon, for twenty years and happily resides with his small family. An unabashed nerd, Karl's spare time is a peculiar cornucopia of computers, comic books, and cardiovascular exercise.

Eight Stories about Teaching I Never Told You

(With thanks to Dan Holt's "Ten Stories about Coyotes
I Never Told You"[5])

Susan Martens

1. Dead Poets' Society

It's movie night in the magic bubble of my freshman year of
college, and I'm having an epiphany watching *Dead Poets' Society*. In
eighth grade, I took a career interest survey, and it told me that I should
be a high school English teacher. Seeing Mr. Keating enchant his posh,
private school students with Romantic poetry cinches the deal for me.
But Mr. Keating joins the cast of characters who embody what I will
eventually deem a dangerous lone-teacher-as-hero mythology. But not
until I use the "barbaric yawp" scene about ten years in a row while
teaching Walt Whitman to high school juniors.

Twenty years later, I note that Mr. Keating lectures a lot and
never uses group work. I wonder if he might also embody Freire's
banking model of education, and I start researching the use of teacher
movies in pre-service English methods courses. I keep thinking about
Nick Nolte's character in *Teachers* and Gabe Kaplan's in *Welcome Back,
Kotter*.

2. Mr. Jonson

I'm back from college on spring break, visiting one of my
favorite teachers from high school. We walk to the commons and sit
near the trophy case at a table with plastic orange chairs—the same
ones, I muse, that I occupied just a year ago. He buys me a soda. I
notice how incredibly, deeply *tired* he looks.

In the 80s, Mr. Jonson was teaching philosophy and political
issues using all the "best practices" of future decades. His room was
arranged in the horseshoe formation, with him sitting with us at one

end of the loop and students talking to each other as much as they talked to him. He asked us to keep reflective journals, and he actually read them. I still have mine, from all three classes I took with him, with those lengthy, witty responses crowding into the margins.

I tell him, proudly, that I am definitely going into teaching. He immediately starts trying to talk me out of it. For the first time, I notice the tension and redness in his eyes. He starts talking about "burnout" in the past tense, deliberately separating the two words and emphasizing them equally. *Burned. Out.* His expression softens a bit, eventually, as he starts talking about getting away to a cabin in the woods, of maybe not coming back.

3. Kevin Andrews

I've stupidly left Kevin, a senior, alone in my windowless classroom for five minutes in after-school detention while I run to the restroom. It's my first year of teaching high school English in this small Midwestern town. When I come back, I notice right away that he has drawn a large, unflattering caricature of me on the marker board. A viciously unflattering caricature, complete with an exaggerated facial mole and stray eyebrow hairs. It stays in my mind forever. I have a vague sense of the even greater pain he has caused other students.

I tell him to erase it and return to his desk. I hold him until the agreed-upon detention time, then let him leave. He takes his place as the first in a mental log of students who I deem, possibly, reluctantly, truly evil. At the very least, anti-social. In twelve years, there are three students on the list, which I share with almost no one.

4. English teacher planet

I'm coming down the escalator into the immense lobby of the Moscone Convention Center. It's my first National Council of Teachers of English convention, and I am utterly amazed. By the fact that my district paid for three English teachers to come to it. But also by the enormity of the crowd, the huge number of concurrent sessions, the multitude of conversations and agendas swirling around us.

"It's like landing on a planet populated entirely by English teachers!" I say as we near the bottom and prepare to merge with the throng.

"Pretty scary," says Chris.

"Terrifying, if you ask me," says Gary.

Both of them are smiling broadly, as am I. There is an overwhelming sensation of recognition, an awareness that These are My People. It is my first sense of myself as part of a wider network. As part of a teaching community. I feel humbled and emboldened and proud all at once.

We keep thinking that we see people we know from Nebraska, but they turn out to be look-alikes. After two days we realize that this phenomenon is due to the fact that there are a number of English teacher archetypes. We begin naming some of them: Elegant Pashmina Woman, Goatee and Glasses Man, Hippy-haired Sandal Person (either gender), Smart Young Professional in Pumps (a.k.a. Conference Shoes). We start wondering which ones we are.

5. The Jackson 5

I'm behind the dusty curtains in the high school gym wearing bell bottoms, a fringy leather vest, and an Afro wig spray painted brown because the only wigs Laura could find were rainbow-colored clown wigs. Three other teachers and the activities director are beside me, similarly attired. We are about to lip-synch and dance to the Jackson Five's song "ABC" for the Writing Pep Rally—one of Chris's many great rogue ideas in her valiant role as School Improvement Coordinator.

As we strut out onto stage and do our teacherly best to shake our groove things, I hazard a glance into the sea of students. Chris would later describe their expressions as a mixture of embarrassment and horror.

Afterwards in class, though, they are good-natured and clearly amused. A member of the dance team says, "You got some moves, Ms. M!"

For five consecutive years after that, my juniors meet their self-determined class goals for passing the statewide writing exam, and I get to spend a day hanging out with them on reward field trips to Omaha's Henry Doorly Zoo. Each year the administration fears for discipline problems, and each year we have none.

6. Tribal paradise project

My friend Jeff, who teaches at a neighboring high school, is in the parking lot of Mahoney State Park, blowing and spitting enthusiastically into a conch shell. He's trying to call our freshmen back from their scavenger hunt, *Lord of the Flies* style. I can see their little heads popping up quizzically from the surrounding trails. They look around, bewildered, then start moving back toward the busses. The sound isn't very loud, but the spectacle of a teacher sputtering into a giant pink shell compels them to band together.

We're finishing up the Tribal Paradise Project, a collaboration between our two schools using the online forums Jeff set up and a *Survivor*-esque approach to a classic novel. The project has pushed logistical limits but gained ground in the digital literacy campaign—an important lesson for me (a relentless planner) in the value of working through glitches and managing chaos with a light hand. And trusting one's colleagues.

I see Jeff's dark head moving above the brightly colored ball caps and tribal banners. After a debate about the acceptability of one group's "spear-making stick," he declares that Red Tribe has won the scavenger hunt. They all cheer, and he uses his speech coach voice to lead the charge toward the park's observation tower.

"Everyone!" he booms triumphantly. "To the snack buffet!"

7. Rainbow flag door vandal

I've had a small rainbow flag sticker on my classroom door for years. The band teacher and I both use them to signal "safe space" for GLBTQ (gay, lesbian, bisexual, transgender and queer) students. But this year—during the Discrimination and Tolerance unit—it disappears. I can't know for certain that someone has ripped it down, but everything else on my classroom door is untouched.

So I make a new one, twice as big, with stickers from the Teaching Tolerance organization, and I put it up with lots and lots of masking tape.

Three days later, it is gone. So I make another one, even bigger, and I put it up with even more masking tape—the really thick kind this time, around the outside edges as well as on the back. It says:

To the person who consistently tears down rainbow symbols in this space:

"Anger and intolerance are the twin enemies of correct understanding."
   –Gandhi

"The highest result of education is tolerance."—Helen Keller

"Ultimately, America's answer to the intolerant man is diversity, the very diversity which our heritage of religious freedom has inspired."
   —Robert Kennedy

"Consistency is the hobgoblin of little minds."—Ralph Waldo Emerson

***

On the last day of school, as I am explaining the essay portion of the final exam in the Discrimination and Tolerance unit, I tell students about the silent dialogue that's been playing out on my classroom door over the last two weeks. I invite them to respond to it, if they like, as part of their writing. I ask them to tell me who is responsible, if they know, and promise that I will not share this information with anyone, not even with the vandal.

No one gives me a name, but many of them apologize sincerely, on behalf of their class, their school, their town. Some take me up on my offer and use the rainbow sticker example in their essays.

Several share stories of gay friends and relatives who have faced ridicule or abuse.

I never find out the name of the vandal, but I find out many other, better things.

8. Moon Over St. Benedict

The whole Platte River valley has become a steam room in the heat and humidity wave, but we are out on the patio nonetheless, drinking wine and spraying ourselves with citronella bug spray that Mary says smells just like Shakespeare on the Green. It's the evening ritual of the annual Nebraska Writing Project Advisory Board retreat at the St. Benedict Retreat Center. We'd spent the day trying to figure out how to keep supporting teachers and students in our programs after the Great Federal Funding Massacre of 2011, so we're a little tired and a little snarly. When it gets late, however, it's hard to break the spell of good company, of teacher stories and not-so-teacher stories traded under the summer stars.

"I'm heading in," I say to the four who remain, gathering up my corkscrew and plastic glasses.

"But the moon is coming up!" says Jeff. He points to a dim glow through the cottonwood trees beyond the fields.

"We *have* to stay up now," says Dan. "Just ten more minutes."

We stand together then, and watch it climb, just-past-full and milky orange in the haze. We even scramble up over some retaining walls to get a better view of it over the statue of St. Benedict in the middle of the lake. In the dark, dewy grass we move this way and that to shift the composition, putting the moon behind his head like a halo, balancing it on the fingers of one of his outstretched arms, letting it hover above his head like an invocation.

"It's so still," says Dan. "I don't think I've ever felt anything so still."

The sound of water lapping against the concrete slides into the night chorus as the moon continues to rise.

❖ ❖ ❖

Susan Martens received a B.A.E. from Wayne State College in Nebraska and an M.A. from the University of South Dakota. She taught high school English/language arts in Nebraska for twelve years before becoming a Ph. D student at the University of Nebraska-Lincoln, where she currently teaches composition and works with pre-service English teachers. She has written for *English Journal* and for the National Writing Project and has presented at national conventions of the NCTE, CCC, AAC&U, Rhetoric Society of America, Popular Culture Association/American Culture Association, and National Writing Project. As a former co-Director of the Nebraska Writing Project, she is the founder and facilitator of writing marathon and writing retreat programs and has co-facilitated several Writing Project Invitational Institutes. She makes her home in Fremont, Nebraska—a base of operations for her ongoing research into place-conscious education and ecological literacy.

Already Behind, No Way to Prepare

Rob La Raus

Teaching means that on your first day of work you walk into a classroom with a coyote skull sitting next to an unfed tarantula because this used to be a science room. It means being assigned to teach four sections of a vaguely titled course, questions about the curriculum of which are met by, "Be creative!" It means spending workdays hiding in your classroom wondering how you could feel this stressed instead of making copies.

Teaching means engaging high school students who lack fifth-grade skills, while classmates two seats over are bored and want extra credit. It means putting hours into a lesson plan only to see it undermined by a fire drill. It means stalking the halls looking for someone, anyone to hear your rant about the absence of a personal finance class in the building. It means hating meetings but struggling to arrange them because students are failing left and right, and society seems to be collapsing daily between 8:30 and 3:35. You know it's bad if meetings even *seem* to be the answer.

Teaching means facing students whose notions of respect are so underdeveloped that they can't quite say what the word means or why they might want it, let alone how hard it is to get. How easy it is to lose someone's respects is a lesson for upperclassmen only.

Teaching means coming back the second year with vastly more realistic expectations. It means having a much better sense of when to push and when to pull, when to step on the gas and when to make goofing off the lesson itself. It means knowing when to sequence the assignments differently, when to let a student fail, and when to take a stand even when a child who simply can't be seen losing face insists on violating the Rule of Holes—if you're already in one, stop digging.

Teaching means getting laid off at the end of the school year, spending the summer looking frantically for work when every district nearby is also laying teachers off. It means getting recalled the day before the new school year begins.

Teaching means seeing colleagues move on without knowing how much you leaned on them. It means not needing to be reminded to focus on the ones who are really trying. It means bumping up expectations and seeing kids meet them, practicing more sophisticated skills than they could last year. It means finally finding the time to be creative and watching kids who hate geometry enthusiastically build gigantic polyhedrons.

Teaching means taking students to places they haven't been and would never go without you. It means gently alerting them to the fact that they are big fish in a small pond. Teaching means letting things go that, before you were a teacher, you would have insisted on clinging to.

Teaching means that some students won't respect you until you insult them, gang affiliations notwithstanding. It means that when one student calls another a moron, and the response is, "You're the moron," you can intervene with something like "Now, now, you're *both* morons" and get a laugh and acceptance of the subsequent redirection. It means discovering that the surly sophomore with the scar under his eye loves fey 80's rock as much as you do. It means being interrupted while explaining alternate interior angles by a student wondering who I pick to win in the UFC tomorrow.

Teaching means working with great people and others who can't seem to get fired no matter how many times a student lights a fire in their classroom. It means district decisions are made, or not made, according to considerations so bizarre you're not sure you've quite woken up, as you reflect upon them. It means periodically screaming, aloud or otherwise, "What are we *doing* here?"

Teaching means doing things for students that have nothing to do with academics because social or emotional considerations are much more significant right now. It means knowing you could spend fifty, sixty, eighty hours every single week reaching out and still not run out of ways to help but drawing the line anyway.

Teaching means being damn proud of what you are trying to accomplish and heartily shaking hands with the stranger who appreciates your effort.

❖ ❖ ❖

Rob La Raus received his B.A. from Cornell College and an M.A.T. from Concordia University in Portland, Oregon, where he lives with his wife and assorted pets. He has taught math at a small alternative high school for five years and hopes to publish a book of vignettes of his experiences there in graphic novel format. "Already Behind, No Way to Prepare" is his first publication.

Reflections of an "Easy Grader"

Joel Shatzky

I was never an "A" student in high school or college. My downfall was always the same: math. It's not that I was unable to "pass" the courses, but I never did really well. Perhaps the problem was my teachers, some of whom didn't seem to realize that their explanations for math problems were difficult for many of my fellow students and me to follow. On the other hand, there were those in my math classes that seemed to have "an aptitude," as it was called, for doing the most complicated algebraic formulas with the ease of an athlete jumping over the hurdles. They had the same teachers I did, were from the same socio-economic background, but they were able to understand easily the logic of the formulas I tried to memorize with limited success. And my inadequacy was despite the fact that both my school teaching parents taught, among other subjects, math.

Ironically, I have always been adept at what is called "numeracy" and can figure out fractions, percentages, and long lists of additions in my head with consistent accuracy. I think one of the reasons for this is that from an early age, I wanted to know the daily change in the batting average of my favorite Yankee, Mickey Mantle, and didn't want to wait for the results in the next day's *New York Post*. As I continued to practice this mental exercise regularly, I found that I had little trouble in other areas of basic arithmetic and continued to become more proficient the older I got.

Some math educators insist that "everybody" can learn algebra and geometry even calculus. And I would like to believe that such is the case, provided, of course, that our educational system would be able to produce enough of the skilled math teachers that can make these disciplines accessible to a larger proportion of students than at present. In fact, finally, in college, when I was taking calculus as a "required" course in my basic studies program, I was taught by a truly skilled instructor, a woman who had been a high school math teacher for many years before going into college teaching. I ended up with my only "D" in college in a course on which I'd spent more time and effort than any other I studied before or since, but I did, at least for a brief time, "understand" the material I was being taught. But that was an exceptional and very painful experience and the only tangible result that I brought out of that class is that I knew I had the perseverance to "get through" a course which, in all other respects, so far as I know, was not useful to me either in terms of general or occupational knowledge.

On the other hand, since I had an incentive to learn percentages in order to follow the fortunes of my favorite ball player, I was continually practicing the mental discipline that I have found very useful for such mundane but practical tasks as figuring out an appropriate tip at a restaurant or checking the total on items rung up at a super market. I was not learning for the sake of a grade or even for my self-esteem.

I make this point because over the years I have come to the conclusion that: There is such a thing as "aptitude" in learning and that, no matter how skillful, teachers do not really teach effectively those students who either do not, or more to the point, cannot, learn certain skills no matter how hard they try.

"Assessing" students through tests, papers, and extensive homework assignments is counterproductive to learning. It's better if the real interests and passions of students are tapped and developed, even when the "subjects" that are learned do not conform to any conventional curriculum.

Many students who do well enough in school to be able to retain, apply, and be innovative with what they have learned in their work, leisure time, and future lives do so in spite of rather than because of their schooling. This is because the paradigm for most schools was established as an industrial model rather than an educationally organic one. The "daily menu" of a typical school day includes an arbitrary amount of time spent on subjects that can be better learned if taught at greater length. The discontinuity that comes with jumping from algebra in period one to French in period two to history in period three with no apparent connections between the disciplines runs counter to what child behaviorists know about the way the youngest learners develop language and other skills. Most curricula have more to do with bookkeeping than substantial learning; "covering the material" rather than understanding it. The level of ignorance of the typical high school or even college-educated graduate of current events, the workings of our political system, basic knowledge of science, not to mention the arts, literature and history, convinces me that no matter the grades students may receive during their "educational experience," only a tiny fraction of what they are taught is understood well enough for them to retain and later apply in their everyday lives.

If one argues that there are many young learners who become outstanding educators, doctors, lawyers, community leaders, and scientists who are a product of education, I would say that it was because they were able to develop strategies of learning that allowed them to negotiate around the obstacles created by the education "system" rather than because of it. And that the most significant learning they experienced was with their peers, and not in the classroom, unless the classroom dynamics had been sufficiently modified to encourage peer learning.

I would suggest, however, that there is one notable exception to these generalities: young learners can be inspired by one of their teachers to apply themselves, not necessarily to learn what is being taught for a grade, but to please the teacher whom they admire. From many anecdotes, I have been able to infer that when former students are asked who their favorite teacher was, they do not recollect so much *what* she taught but rather *how* she taught.

An example is a recent e-mail I received from a student I had taught thirty years ago who found an article I had written on-line and was able to contact me. I received the following in May of 2011:

Mr. Shatzky,

I was a class of '81 math major and I took your Science Fiction class in the Spring semester of 81. . . . I know that single class from you has stayed with me all these years. I reread Brave New World this summer. I am sure that we read it and Stranger in a Strange Land among others that I cannot remember. I am pretty sure that you wrote a reference for my Peace Corps application. I know that we exchanged letters while I was in Liberia and that we visited in your office at Cortland when I returned home. I do not expect you to remember me among your thousands of students, but whether you do or not, I know you left a lasting impression on me.

It seems to me that what has given him "a lasting impression" is the way I taught rather than what. Today, as I teach students as a semi-retired adjunct at a community college, I find that it is my ability to "connect" with the students that is my most effective teaching tool regardless of the specific material they are studying. I know that many of them will be unlikely to recall in detail a single essay we read in class or the short story we analyzed, but they just might remember my enthusiasm in teaching and, more important, my interest in them that might have motivated them to be more careful readers, and broadly interested in learning more than what they needed to get by in their jobs.

***

All of this is preamble to what for others might be a "confession:" I am what most students might call an "easy grader." I make it clear in my class that if they do the work and get to a certain level of proficiency through revision, they could all receive an "A" in the class. And I do this with the full awareness that, by most standards, some students will deserve an "A" more than others. It is my way to protest what I feel is the idiocy of grading students for their work instead of describing what they do. But I believe, as Alfie Kohn has extensively written in many of his studies on educational practices: grades not only do not improve student learning; they often retard it.[6]

But rather than attempt to defend my practice—I do give an NG (no grade) when I see a student isn't trying but they then have an opportunity to get an "A" by doing their best—I would like to offer my suggestions for ways to improve learning without recourse to using grades.

Although in the past, at least when I was growing up in the 1950s, there was a rough balance between the objectives of education being "learning for its own sake" and "getting a job," the former is rarely mentioned nearly as much today as the latter. When President Obama talks about education, he urges that our country step up to the challenges of "global competition" even though a lot of the "globe" is dominated by multi-national corporations based in the U.S. and the "competition" that these corporations are engaged in is to find ways of employing high-skilled workers at lower wages. This is certainly to the detriment of students who believe a college degree will give them a good-paying job. Thus, one of the initial objectives of such educators as John Dewey, to improve the education system in order to have an "informed electorate" is being downplayed in the interest of "skilling" rather than educating young learners.

Second of all, the "crisis" in our schools has been going on for fifty years, only it is far less an educational crisis than an economic one. In the past, a student could legally leave school at sixteen, if not younger, get a decent-paying job, and might be able to make good money by the time he or she reached twenty. Most of those jobs are gone, and the students who are now a large proportion of the "slow learners" or "discipline problems" in the past years would have found a suitable job and not a meaningless—for them—non-educational experience. Back in those days, some of these ex-students would return to finish their high school degree and even move forward to higher aspirations with the wisdom of experience.

With the mandatory attendance policy enforced today, by the time they leave, they might never want to go to school again.

But, I believe, there are a number of measures that can improve the opportunities for students to actually learn and grading has no part of them.

1. Many students learn better later in the day than early morning. Delaying the opening times of classes has improved learning at a number of schools in various parts of the country among high school students.[7]

2. The physical arrangement of the school space can have a positive effect on the atmosphere for learning. This would involve abandoning the box-like classroom structure and constructing more open spaces, greater exposure to natural light, and a more informal atmosphere.

3. Although it would require careful planning and scrupulous attention to effectiveness, educational

strategies should move from "subject centered" to "project centered" learning since knowledge is fundamentally interdisciplinary. I can anticipate many objections to this approach, but I would defend it by suggesting that the necessary learning needed to fulfill the demands of project-oriented work would be more substantially retained and applied later in students' lives than what often is reflected at present in the massive ignorance of the American public about what it was supposed to have learned in school.

4. Although it can be very poorly done, collaborative learning—exemplified in science labs—can be much more effective in motivating and bringing out best efforts in students than the isolated "knowledge-hoarding" in which competition for grades becomes the norm, and a relatively few students actually thrive because of it.

5. Although I can see many positive uses for technology in instruction, the trend has been for school districts to use them as a substitute for live teaching as a cost-saving measure. This, again, like so many strategies to reduce the human factor in teaching, will be successful for those students who will find ways around these obstacles to real learning and leave behind those with a lower level of motivation and ability to learn. Technology should be judiciously used, but, for the most part, as a supplement to learning before and after regular class time.

6. While the practical aspect of education is very important for most students, such emphasis must be tempered with the more humanistic values that should be a part of any student's life: art, music, theatre, dance and other so-called "frills" which often provide more interest, engagement and motivation to learn than many of the "practical"

courses which might be less accessible to them. Teaching math and music, history and art, chemistry and literature through team teaching can have fruitful results.

7. It's important for students to feel that their teachers actually care about them, so some level of personal concern should be encouraged. Just because there are instances of predatory behavior on the part of a tiny fraction of teachers, the overwhelming majority of teachers are geared to be nurturers if given the opportunity. This does not mean that everyone can become a "Mr. Chips" or start a "Dead Poet's Society," but the idea that teachers must be dispassionate and detached from their students as a matter of policy strikes me as another example of backward pedagogy. Students who believe that their efforts matter to their teachers are more likely to put in the necessary commitment to do their best than if they feel alienated by "professional" indifference.

8. Although mentioned last, the most important measure, especially in the present atmosphere of test mania, is to reduce or eliminate the forms of metrically deterministic "tests" of student learning. Generally, the purpose of high-stakes testing and grading is not to encourage and advance learning, but rather to "sort" students for the benefit of corporate convenience, especially when well-paying jobs are at a premium and elite schools have dozens of applications for every slot. There is no certain way of determining how well students can perform through other forms of evaluation such as projects and portfolios, but I would argue that using testing and grading by itself as a means to encourage students' best efforts runs counter to all I know about how and why students want to learn.

Unfortunately, there are children who, for many reasons, including poverty, unfamiliarity with English, and learning disabilities, are less able to learn as readily as their classmates. But, if they are not as easily teachable, even using the most effective progressive techniques, they should not be doomed to a life of poverty just because our entrepreneurial culture seems incapable of producing a sufficient number of adequate-paying jobs to sustain most workers in this the richest Third-world economic system on the planet.

***

I may be an "easy grader" to many of my students, but I can see from their work when they are trying and when they have given up. Giving a student a D- on a paper and then offering the "opportunity" for her to write an "A" paper in order to get a "C" to me does not make sense. Giving each student an "A" if they are willing to do their best work, even if it isn't as good as someone else's, will motivate those who most likely have been discouraged in the past by poor grades until they are no longer worrying about the grades. What I try to do is get them "beyond grades."

As for the "standards" that are being debated today; they will not produce any better results than at present until there are a lot of drastic reforms in, not just our educational system, but also our economic system. Trying to do the one without the other is like trying to get a car without an engine to run by putting on new tires.

To let you know how I practice what I preach, I teach a course on the short story at my community college and tell each student that, in order to get an "A," they need to write a short story of their own. Students "brainstorm" through multiple drafts and complete work by a deadline since they know that the stories will be professionally printed, and each student will receive a copy of the anthology at the end of the semester. I have gotten almost total compliance from my students who finally have the opportunity to "own" what they chose to learn, not have it dictated from "above." Getting the "A" no longer is the main issue: getting your own work published is.

Of course, there are many other strategies that can be used to enable students to "own their work."

Testing and grading are "owned" by bureaucrats.

Joel Shatzky is a retired college professor who still teaches English by working as an adjunct at Kingsborough Community College (CUNY). Prior to that, he taught at SUNY—Cortland from 1968-2005. He has degrees in English, including a B.A. from Queens College, an M.A. from the University of Chicago, and a Ph.D. from New York University. His dozens of publications include: *The Thinking Crisis* (with Ellen Hill), *Contemporary Jewish-American Authors*, and *Contemporary Jewish-American Dramatists and Poets*. A Bronx native, Shatzky, who lost his first wife, Dorothy, to cancer, now lives in Brooklyn and has since remarried to Ilana Abramovitch, who teaches Jewish Studies at Brooklyn College (CUNY). His son, Ben, is a lawyer who lives in Queens and is married to Betty Estacio; they have a daughter, Sophia. Shatzky's daughter, Judy, is a social worker living in Brooklyn. Shatzky contributes a regular column, "Educating for Democracy," to the Huffington Post.

Teaching is Activism

Danielle Helzer

Abusive parents, feelings of abandonment, serious illnesses, death, stories of kids growing up way too fast, pressure to fit in, court cases, unhealthy relationships.

***

I just finished reading a batch of student journals. Of course these heavy topics were sprinkled among entries about golf tournaments, learners permits, life philosophies, to-do lists, drawings of spaceships and talking pizzas, song lyrics, and other light-hearted subjects. But it's the weighty entries that drive me to tears at my kitchen table with my pen lingering over the paper, as I try to come up with a set of soothing words to comfort each student. Somehow, "I'm sorry you have to deal with all of this. You shouldn't have to. Keep your head high and hold on to hope. If you ever need to talk, my door is open" just seems shallow and contrived. These stories give me a glimpse of the lives they live outside my classroom; they keep me up late at night as I mull over what I should've done better to let each student know I care. Most of all, these journals and the students behind them remind me that to teach is to be an activist—an advocate for students who places more value on them rather than their test scores.

District and state assessments tell me very little about my students. They can't tell me how they learn best; they don't provide me with an accurate measure of their ability to think critically. Assessments can't show how far one student has come in learning to control his anger. They can't tell me that having to work until one in the morning the night before in order to help provide for the family may be why they failed that particular test. My students are so much more than their test scores. They are creative, complex, quirky individuals with stories to tell.

***

When I began teaching, I thought I'd just be filling students' heads with knowledge about writing and literature. I didn't realize I'd have to teach students how to be good people; I thought that was up to the parents. Nobody told me that teaching is largely activism—campaigning for students' best interests. I assumed everyone involved in education did the right thing. I always thought I'd retire as a teacher.

But now I'm not so sure. I love my job; I love my students. But I'm unsure how much longer I can keep fighting the powers that be, giving so much of my life to students. I've heard that the life of an English teacher is five years, and, after year three, I believe it. I've had it set in my mind that I'd do something different in five years—I'd go back to school full time to pursue a Ph.D., so I don't have to deal with the hassles that sometimes come with being a public school teacher, or, better yet, I'd land an office job that requires no after-hours work.

***

But if teaching is activism, then it's also service. And sometimes service sucks. Serving others isn't glamorous. It's not an 8 to 5 job. Serving sometimes requires us to get dirty and wash grimy feet—to humble ourselves. After reading those journals (even though it took me two hours to read twenty-four out of seventy-five), I feel like I can't give up. My students need me to be there for them because I may be the only adult in their lives who actually cares. I need them to teach me empathy and to look beyond myself. I can't give up the responsibility I have to fight through the exhaustion, put my selfish desires aside, and work to give each kid a chance.

***

Unfortunately, many are leaving or will leave the education profession. Some do so because they're not cut out for it, while others will leave because politicians will push them out with their requirements to teach to a test, rather than teach to the student. With this expectation, many students will not have the chance to think critically or develop a habit of inquiry. Discussing issues that matter to society and then acting to make a true impact on communities aren't priorities when teaching to a test. If I changed my teaching methods to align with these expectations, my twelfth graders wouldn't get to research and blog about socially relevant topics, sharing and pushing one another to go beyond the obvious. My ninth graders wouldn't have the chance to apply Dr. Martin Luther King Junior's four non-violent steps to direct action, as they committed themselves to make an impact on our community. The family in Keystone, Nebraska, would not have received over $900 to help pay medical bills all raised from a soup supper organized by a fourteen and fifteen year old. The Keith and Arthur County Food Pantry would have 200 less items. Not only would my students be robbed of these rich experiences that a textbook alone simply couldn't provide, my community would suffer.

***

Though it's emotionally and physically draining to teach in a day and age where teachers are not respected and students are treated as test-taking-robots, I'll stick with education for as long as possible. I'll take interest in students beyond their test scores; I'll fight to give them a chance.

Danielle Helzer received a B.A. in language arts education from the University of Nebraska at Kearney and is pursuing an M.A. in English and teaching from the University of Nebraska at Lincoln. She is in her fourth year of teaching high school language arts. Currently, she teaches and coaches at Ogallala High School in Ogallala, Nebraska, where she lives with her husband, who is also a teacher. In addition to teaching, Danielle serves as a board member for the Nebraska Writing Project, maintains a professional learning network blog for her school district, and has presented several workshops at both the state and national level in order to support the use of effective technology incorporation into the classroom.

We Know

Erin Parker

In February 2011, Wisconsin Governor Scott Walker and the Republican majority in the State Assembly and Senate proposed legislation that would eliminate collective bargaining rights for state employees and public school teachers. Teachers, students, and the public congregated at the Capitol building in Madison to protest. Students from the local schools staged mass walkouts, and the school district closed for four days. At the time of this writing, the proposed legislation has been passed, and efforts are underway to recall both the governor and several members of the legislature.

We know we don't know everything. We know feeling like we don't know anything. But we know so much. We know our students and their families. We know the ones who don't have enough, and we know the ones who have too much. We know who woke up late, who broke up with whom, who broke into someone's apartment. We know late nights. We know janitors because we stay at school so late, so often. We know secretaries, because they know everything. We know cheating. We know studying. We know how many hours it takes to put together a lesson, and we know we don't want to grade anymore. We know taking work home nights and weekends, those summers "off" when we take second jobs and continuing education credits. We know we can't sleep because we can't let go. We know we should stop teaching when we're able to let go. We know we save all the things our students give us—artwork, rap lyrics, flowers. We know lost assignments and missed deadlines, and we know disorganization. We know messy backpacks, lockers, lifestyles. We know frustration. We know "Fuck you!" and "Thank you!" And we know we're probably doing something right if we hear them in a two-to-one ratio.

***

We know that the student who was murdered at the end of the year deserved more. We know that most of our pregnant students didn't finish high school. We know one of them just graduated. We know jail sentences and college admittances. We know our students' needs can be overwhelming, and their successes can be thrilling.

***

We know anger. We know injustice. We know inequity, inequality, and achievement gaps. We know whining. We know coaching and advising and field trips; we know paying for things that our students can't afford. We know buying things we don't really want because our students are selling them. We know giving up lunch hours and lunches. We know hearing things that make us laugh until we cry. We know our hearts cracked open by their stories.

***

We know content. We know pedagogy. We know inquiry, constructivism, best practices. We know data driven. We know No Child Left Behind. We know jargon. We know our kids are amazing. We know the truth and work behind "we're here for the children."

***

We know crying in front of our second hour class because that lumbering sophomore, with poor hygiene and seeming disinterest, hugs us in front of everyone and says, "I'm walking out, today, for you and for all of my teachers." We know the two-mile walk from the front steps of school to downtown. We know kids walking those two miles six days in a row. We know those two miles, too. We know the night we stayed at the Capitol until four in the morning because our students signed up to speak, and we wouldn't leave, we couldn't leave until they spoke. And we cried then, too, when they spoke because it was powerful to watch other people listening to our students. We know pride. We know walking our students home because it was four in the morning, and we know working at eight that day and crying again because our coworkers were so haggard and bewildered. We know students carrying a sign that said "We love our teachers." And we know it had our names written on it. We know our students change, and we know they change us, too.

***

We know that we shouldn't give out cell phone numbers because we know they'll call. We know we do it anyway because, sometimes, we know they need more help. We know sleepless nights and social workers. We know IEP meetings. We know principals and central administration. We know exhaustion. We know it will never be enough, and we know we'll never stop trying. We know the way it feels in September, and the way it feels in June. We know rules made by people who don't teach generally don't work. We know we'll fight for our kids. We know that it takes so much more to be a teacher than we can ever put into words. We know that, if you don't teach, you'll never really understand these stories. We know.

Erin Parker received her B.S. in ecology from Michigan Technological University and multiple teaching certifications from Edgewood College. She currently teaches high school Earth sciences at Madison East High School in Madison, Wisconsin, where she works hard to emphasize reading, writing, and communicating along with the science content. As a lifelong dabbler in writing, she was thrilled to participate in the first cohort of the Greater Madison Writing Project in the summer of 2011. From writing yearbook copy in high school to working as a learning coach in the Michigan Technological University writing center as an undergraduate to supporting student writing in the classroom, she remains enamored with, and committed to, the art and science of communicating through the written word.

Boxes

Bruce Greene

The boxes bother no one. My classes meet for the final two weeks, and students either move or sit on the boxes. Tomorrow we pack up the bigger books. The wall of cardboard will rise and those boxes will not move as easily.

There is no lesson plan for the last days of a sixty-five year-old high school. In three weeks, my classroom, like the entire school, will be dust and, then, air. We're being shipped off to a temporary campus for a few years. Never having seen the death of a high school before, our emotions are mixed at best, confused at worst. How do I put my professional life in boxes? What goes? What stays? What cannot be boxed?

When the final class ends, the last boxes join the pile. Like the all the rest, they are marked with a red or green label. The green tagged boxes will appear in a temporary classroom on a campus students have already re-named Guantanamo High School. An internment camp of portables. No hallways, no cafeteria, no gym, no grass quads, no history. The red-tagged boxes will be trashed. They will die a crushing death in the largest dumpsters I have ever seen. Dumpsters that hold more than the studio I rented thirty-five years earlier when I began teaching. They contain what cannot be saved, what cannot be recycled, what did not stand the test of time. Broken staplers, deteriorating projects from our Museum of Living Literature, crippled desks, dried up markers, broken crayon nubs, chalk erasers with no more mileage, dried, caked, glue bottles, glue sticks, glue dispensers. Useless stereo speakers, a broken CD player, archaic army-green file cabinets, miscellaneous plastic chess pieces, abandoned notebooks, worn out clothing, all end up in red-tagged boxes. We are encouraged not to think too long about saving anything.

The boxes lining the wall contain what I will keep. Many have books: sets of novels, dictionaries, biographies, poetry, psychology textbooks, and a classroom library of 300 titles carefully developed through four decades. Like most teachers I know, I, too, subsidize my own classroom. Two boxes have what no casual observer could ever imagine. They hold what those who have not been consumed by cynicism, and understand the value and reality of public education would save. They contain what teachers who have experienced the joy that occasionally thrives in even the most under-resourced environments could save. These boxes house what could never be labeled, sorted, or replaced. Packed in these boxes is a small ceramic plant from Emily, a refugee from Asian girl gangs, who wanted me to know I gave her something to think about. The Korean wall hangings from Park, struggling to learn English, living alone in a strange country after his father gave him one-way plane ticket and enough money to rent an apartment for one month. "You go and be educated," he told his son. He worked eight hours daily at a video rental store, made enough to continue paying rent and eat. Beneath the fragile Chinese paper cuts from Jin are poems from Beret, a plastic bag of hard candies for diabetic emergencies, a new South African flag from Benny and a recipe for tamales from the Gutierrez twins. Two large manila envelopes are in the lightest box. They contain a collection of thank you notes, personal messages, and a few more objects. Some detail all manner of family emergencies. A coffee cup with MR. GREENE carved on the earthy pigment from the student whose father mysteriously snapped one day and killed his mother and sister before surrendering his own life to a SWAT team. "Thank you for helping me cope with this difficult situation." Prom pictures. Happy couples. Uncomfortable couples. Improbable couples. (The transsexual prom queen wearing half a tux and half a gown.)

Near the end, I spend time with my classroom. Many of the green boxes have been taken to their new home. I pause and decide to lock the door anyway. With me is one last box. Here, I have carefully placed the documentation of burgeoning attempts to privatize public education. Here lie the forced assessments I resisted, the skewed data so idolized by misinformed politicians and opportunists, the intellectualized teacher-bashing research of the uninitiated, the vestiges of reform that only spells L-O-C-K-S-T-E-P.

***

This box I bury in the super-sized dumpster. With thirty-two years in the books, I can afford to stand up. I can report that I do not dread coming to work, that a love of learning must be carefully cultivated. That teachers assess daily, not just with standardized tests.

This is my ritual. The last rites. Rain begins to fall, then pounds, while I place this cardboard coffin deep in the pile. What cannot be boxed is that, in my classroom, all who enter are urged to take risks and think deeply. I glance at the abandoned schoolyard with last night's graffiti suddenly meaningless. But there is other writing on other walls. I remind myself that so much of teaching is like planting seeds. Time to watch them grow.

Bruce Greene received his B.A. from U.C.L.A. and his secondary teaching certification from U.C. Berkeley. He taught high school English, history, and psychology in the Bay Area for many years. As a teacher/consultant for the Bay Area Writing Project and Oregon Writing Project, Bruce has developed and offered a variety of workshops. He now supervises and mentors beginning teachers at Marylhurst University, near Portland, Oregon, where he lives with his wife, Katie. In his eclectic writing career, he has been a correspondent for a national thoroughbred horse magazine and published everything from poetry to educational research on his own practice, as well as creative non-fiction and memoir. He is a founding member of The Guttery, a Portland-based writing group. Read his memoir, *Above This Wall: The Life and Times of a VISTA Volunteer 1969-70,* at *http://lifeandtimesofvista.blogspot.com*

Teaching Means Confronting Desperation

This is Where We Come From

Lauren Gatti

"Lee and Ira are coming in," my boss at the restaurant explains to me early on a Friday night shift. "Their oldest son died this week." Larry talks to me through the kitchen window, not looking up. He pushes a steaming plate into the window, meets my gaze. His hazel green eyes are focused and intense; his brow sweating from the heat in the kitchen. He drags a forearm across it, continues: "Thirty-seven years old. Lung cancer. Wasn't even a smoker. We'll send them food. Lee, she likes the pizza. And the Zuppa. And we'll get them dessert." They are good friends of his, in from Arizona for the services. Larry will cook for them. "Come into the restaurant," he had told Ira on the phone the day of the funeral. "You need to eat for God's sake."

You see all kinds when you're waitressing: fashionistas in their Seven jeans and crocodile pumps floating in a cloud of daylilies and patchouli; the couples who fight silently at the table, the bubbling anger just below the surface, each jab cloaked in the polite wool of etiquette. You watch first dates, last dates, the engagements. You witness women across from empty chairs waiting uncomfortably while their food gets cold, their boyfriend outside making a thirty-minute business call. You endure the out-of-towners who drink White Zinfandel, ask for chicken parmesan, and tip ten percent; the cocky businessmen who thrust their hand in your face and demand, without looking at you, "Come back in ten minutes." And then there are the regulars, the people who make you feel good for still being around. The people who ask for you when they call to make reservations or who include you in their pictures or gush because you have the same name as their daughter—one-year-old and beautiful.

***

It is an intimate experience, waiting on people. You see them clearly and honestly because they, for all intents and purposes, do not see you. By the end of a meal, you generally understand what they like and how they like it—more than many of their friends or co-workers might know about them. And, if you have waited on the same people before, you have a different kind of intimacy. You can anticipate their needs, their special orders. You know, for example, that Marty and Christine will order a bottle of Chianti Classico, that they want the pizza regardless of what's on it. They like crushed red pepper and their bread pudding with extra caramel. You feel a part of their lives on a micro level. You know what they want.

And this is no small thing.

***

Lee and Ira I have waited on before. I know that he likes a Grey Goose martini extra cold, up with olives, that she will have one glass of Shiraz Cabernet. Larry knows that she does not like artichokes, so, when they order the pizza tonight, he will make a special one without them. And they know their part. They know, for example, that Larry will always send dessert. So we go through the ritual together; I bring the dessert menus, they gush and drool over the things that they want but have no room for, and order nothing, knowing that I will communicate to Larry what they want, and that he will have the pleasure of sending it out to them. On the house. The script is comforting, and you cannot deviate.

It is a learned talent to know if and when to share something about yourself at a table or to inquire or quip or joke with them. Talk too much about yourself or become too familiar, and you have disrupted the balance between server and patron. You are not, after all, a part of their meal. You are the facilitator. Sometimes the last thing a table needs is to feel the pressure of talking to you. Especially if you are waiting on them the day they have buried their son.

***

I am not married, and I do not have children, but I have buried a child. Several years ago at the Chicago high school where I taught during the week, one of my favorite students was shot and killed by a rival gang member. Whether Sergio himself was in a gang or if it was simply his connection to his brother and his brother's friends, who were in a gang, was never established. Nonetheless, at 3:23 A.M. on Sunday, March 23, a bullet ripped through his young body, killing him. He grunted two words, it was said, to the boy who held him as he died: "It hurts."

***

The day after Sergio is killed, I walk into my classroom where twenty-six of Sergio's peers are sitting, shell-shocked and speechless. Boys and girls have their heads on the desks; others are staring ahead or looking down, not bothering to wipe their tears. Eliana simply walks out of the classroom, only to return with Kleenex. She gives me two before she hands them off to be passed around. No one speaks. Later that day, when attempting to hold it together to give a test to my freshman, I break. I am in the middle of a word, and I cannot continue. Standing at the podium, I place my head in my hands. My eyes are closed, and I cannot breathe. When I finally look up, trying desperately to pull it together, I see their faces looking at me. They are patient and respectful; they understand this moment. "Don't worry, Miss. Take your time," Maria says from the front of the room, her huge brown eyes comforting. *It's all right, Miss. Cry.*

The day of the funeral, I am sitting on the floor in the front of the cramped bus. There is no music, and no one speaks. Jaime looks out the window. Nacho has his head on the person next to him. Clarisia has her eyes closed, her elbow on the window, her hand on her forehead. I see shards of the neighborhoods through which we are passing through the bus doors. Neighborhoods I have never seen on the west side of Chicago—the Chicago bungalows with their cramped lawns and identical spaces; gang graffiti trying desperately to cancel each other out; long urban roads that stretch out endlessly, an urban treadmill. Many of my students are from these neighborhoods, and, on this day, driving through them with my stunned students, I feel like I am being initiated. *This is where we come from Miss.* I am a guest, a witness.

I have never been at a real burial—where you see the casket being lowered into the ground, and where the last thing you do is throw flowers on the casket before the bulldozer standing nearby dumps dirt into the hole. There are no illusions here about what is happening to this child. He is dead, and he is being buried. He is in the ground. I cannot shake the feeling that he is being buried alive, and I fight the feeling to say something, anything, to stop them. So, I am relieved when Adriana tells me that she needs to find a bathroom. Her high heels make it very hard for her to walk, which, given how badly she needs to use the bathroom, adds to the urgency of the situation. We are navigating a dirt path to the mausoleum. She is desperate, stopping every few feet, crossing her legs. I am trying to comfort her: "It's okay, Adriana. We'll find one. Worst case scenario, you go in the bushes." We separate and try to find a bathroom in this quiet marble structure, and, of course, there is none. This place is for the dead, not the living. She is panicking, almost in tears, and I give her Kleenex, point her to bushes on the side of the road. "No one will see you, Adriana. Just go." When she returns, and we are hobbling back to the gravesite, we do not speak. All formalities and conventions are done with.

Alma had the idea of buying seventeen balloons—one for each year of Sergio's life, and one for each member of our *asesoria* (advisory). After the funeral, we stand out on the plaza. It is a painfully bright March day. We are exhausted and floating. We pass around markers to write on our balloon, each writing a personal message to Sergio. When we are ready, we let them go, these red and blue and green bulbs lifting themselves slowly, rising like bread, like grief offered up. Adults would be beyond this kind of symbolic gesture, but these kids are not, and I am amazed that this small act makes my letting go of Sergio real. There are seventeen balloons in the wind blowing somewhere beyond Chicago. There are seventeen years in the wind blowing somewhere beyond Chicago. I watch my balloon until there is nothing but sky. Cheryl sees my swollen eyes, sees that I cannot stop crying, and she hugs me. "It's okay, Miss." It is too beautiful a day to bury someone, I think. Seventeen years, I think.

***

At the restaurant, though, things are different. I do not, with Ira and Lee, acknowledge verbally what has happened to them. I respect the luxury of being emotionally anonymous—no need to respond or to be felt sorry for in public. I am at their table, reciting specials and taking orders and bringing bread, but my mind is with them in the funeral home, in the hospital. I know that the dead animate themselves in the minds of the living, refashioning fantastic sets out of the flimsy fiber that was memory, abandoned. I imagine that their tired minds are bloated, grown immense with these memories, the hum of a son who whispers and lingers. He colors each black and white thing as he moves through it. The pool that caught his first dive explodes into blue; the yellow sun bursts into color. Or the way he blushed the first time they caught him lying, his thin facing bleeding red inside the young skin. Technicolor. They had almost forgotten.

Or perhaps, they are past this for today, perhaps they are saying to their son, *No. No more just now. We are hungry and tired.* Or maybe they are thinking nothing. Simply eating.

***

I remember watching Sergio's father at the mass the school had for Sergio. He stood next to his wife and looked strangely out of place given that he was the father. I imagine that he, like Ira at the restaurant, was not in the church at that moment. Maybe he was at Sergio's side the night he was killed. Maybe he was there with his son saying, *It's okay, son, let go. I know it hurts.* Or maybe he was saying, *Don't go. You can't go. Everything I have sacrificed, I have sacrificed for you. You cannot leave me here in this country alone.*

How do fathers grieve their sons? How do they bury the boy they created, the young man who was supposed to do what they could not? The boy they risked their life for, the one they crossed the border for? The young man who had the courage they did not, the profile they did not, the humor they did not, the fate they did not. All of these things, recessive genes that skipped them. They would gladly change their blood if it meant that they could keep him.

In the church that day, I say nothing to Sergio's father, my Spanish weak, and my courage flagging. And what would I have said, after all?

***

But I look at Lee and Ira. *I will bring you food.* I think. *I will keep the drinks coming. Today is the only day that you can say:* Today I buried my oldest son. *Everything I bring you is a prayer.*

After they pay their bill, and I see Ira has tipped me 100%. I see them on their way out. Ira does not look at me, but takes my arm, his smooth hand on my elbow. He pats me awkwardly with his other hand, looking straight ahead down the ramp and out the door.

"Thanks," he says. I watch him walk away, and I feel overwhelmed, emotional. I was only his waitress. He will not remember me. But I have been a part of the worst day of his life. And I have brought them food.

Lauren Gatti received a B.A. in English from Lawrence University in Appleton, Wisconsin, and an M.A. in English from Loyola University of Chicago. She taught high school English in and around Chicago for eleven years before she began her doctoral studies in curriculum and instruction at the University of Wisconsin-Madison. In the summer of 2011, she was selected to participate in the Greater Madison Writing Project's first Summer Institute. Currently, she teaches a course in college composition and is completing her dissertation, which explores how novice English teachers are learning to teach English and facilitate discussion in urban contexts. Her poetry has been published in *The Willow Review*, and her academic work has been published in *English Journal* and *Teacher Education and Practice*.

It's On Me

Charley Barniskis

I stop Nate before first period and ask, "Whoa, what happened to your cheek?"

His shiny, swollen left eye looks at the light switch to my right. Stale smoke leaks from the battleship grey Metallica T-shirt that clings only to his shoulders. "Nothing," he mumbles. His eyes crawl up to my right shoulder, and he asks, "Can I go to my locker?"

I straighten up my shoulders as I take a deep breath. I can feel the weight of the doorjamb push on my spine, a firm gravity. I look at his battered blue notebook and eraser-less pencil dangling at his side.

I focus my eyes on his forehead and ask, "What do you need, Nate?"

He glances at the windows and says, "Somethin'."

The bell rings. We hover in the doorframe: one foot in the classroom, the other in the hallway. His eyes finally find my gaze, and I nod.

He says "thanks," and I walk into the room alone; twenty-nine other students wait for "somethin'" from me. Immediately:

"Can you please not take each other's stuff, even if it's a joke?"

"Has anyone seen a green overhead marker?"

"You did a nice job in class discussion yesterday."

"Can you take the iPod earphones out?"

"No one else is going to the bathroom for now so please stop asking."

"Are you feeling better today?"

"Yes, you can go get your book from your locker."

"I'm sorry your printer was not working again, but I still need your essay."

"I hope that you can find something useful in this book even if you don't like it. We are reading it for the BIG ideas is contains."

"I don't know why he thought Mark Twain was a better name than Samuel Clemons."

"Did you see your dad this weekend? How did it go?"

"Are you caught up on your reading now?"

"Please put your cell phone away."

I breathe deeply…and wonder about Nate.

At the podium, I open to the section of *The Adventures of Huckleberry Finn* that includes Huck's description of his time with Pap in the cabin by the river: "But by and by pap got too handy with his hick'ry, and I couldn't stand it. I was all over welts." Huck's dad hopes to get the treasure he and Tom Sawyer found and is tired of Huck not listening to him. And people wonder why it is so remarkable that Huck develops a sense of morality, however imperfect, from such circumstances. I clear my throat to read aloud and glance at the window. Nate is getting into a beat-up blue Civic with Wesley from fourth period. Through the open window, Nate raises his birch-branch thin and bruised arm and waves.

He is absent the next day. I keep Wesley back at the end of fourth period. He tells me that the previous day they went to breakfast—Wesley's treat. And Nate "devoured, like, two Lumberjack omelets and three glasses of orange juice." Wesley pauses, gazes at the front of my desk, and asks, "Are you gonna do anything?"

The desks are empty. My eyes find the light switch to his left. I nod, somewhere between somethin' and nothin'.

Charley Barniskis received his B.A. in English from the University of Wisconsin and his M.Ed. from the University of Minnesota. He taught for three years at Sandy High School in Sandy, Oregon. For the past nine years, he has taught at Minnetonka High School in Minnetonka, Minnesota. His wife is also a high school English teacher, while his son is a professional four-year-old. Charley participated in the Minnesota Writing Project in 2010 and is a member of their advisory board.

Some Bunny Loves You

Janin Spoor

It sat there, on my desk, dirty and crusted over from years of drool, food and beverages that the soft fur had soaked up. The left ear looked as if it had been chewed by some animal in the wild. You could discern that at one time the blue fluff had been a pleasant hue; a comfort to some tiny body, while being squeezed and snuggled. Some heart had loved the smelly, threadbare bunny into a caricature of the children's tale, "The Velveteen Rabbit."

As I picked up the offending misplaced toy, a warbled squeaky voice exclaimed, "Some bunny loves you!" I am starting to fear that this was not placed on my desk by mistake. Working in an impoverished area, I was becoming used to "gifts" from giant-hearted children that had been carefully selected from the "Everything's Ninety-Eight Cents" store. While my colleague, Sandra, had at one time gotten a used, lacy nightgown from an adoring little girl, sure that it would make her teacher as beautiful as her mother, this was my first foray into the "gently" used category of prizes.

Looking at the faces around the classroom, those, "how can they be that big" fifth graders became children in my mind again. Baby faces with breakfast still on their cheeks, legs kicking with uncontrollable energy, happy to be at school, where they are safe and valued.

My first class. My first journey into a career I didn't even want but fell into and sometimes resented. This was not the dream class I had imagined in my training. These children did not come from the hills of the Valley, teeming with privilege and excess. They didn't even come from the nice apartments and rented houses of the middle class in Los Angeles, close to city centers of opportunity. These children, babies, came from what can only be referred to as tenements. Surrounded by barbed wire and security gates that don't work, broken down, cramped and void of freshness, these places of their childhoods, had me locking the car door and rolling the windows up tight.

With my upbringing that stressed importance of social justice, here I was witnessing how, sometimes, life goes on in spite of the injustice around it. These grandchildren of the original gangster had a resiliency that can only be described as one of those trick birthday candles, you can keep blowing, but the flame won't go out.

But still, "some bunny loves you" rings out from my desk, and the unexpected boy appears at my side. The smallest boy in class, Jose had an attitude that makes up for his stature. We had been locking horns all year. His inability to stay seated, his disrespect, his temper, his lack of effort, and lack of completed homework all culminated in my frustration. And after trying all of my reasonable, new teacher strategies, I was becoming unreasonable. I found myself purple in the face with anger, pounding on my desk to try and formulate some sort of impression. I even threatened several more years of fifth grade to come. Eventually, I found out later that, with "social promotion," these threats were very empty.

It was only after the worst day ever that I came to the stunning illumination that I was only focusing on his faults and not my own. I had not taken the time to get to know Jose. I had not investigated the scars on his psyche, the reason behind his rocky, hard exterior. Not until one of our many clashes had Jose curled up in the fetal position beneath his desk, whispering about how he preferred to be dead, was I stopped cold, my soul chilled. How, at ten years old, does a child think of death as a preference to school? Was I somehow the catalyst for this boy's desire for death?

I immediately softened like butter left out overnight. Scooting the rest of the class out to recess, I ignored every warning given to teachers and very humanely scooped little Jose up and sat him in the chair facing mine. Looking into his hard brown eyes, hot with tears, I asked for a truce. I asked for redemption. I asked for a chance to get to know this little boy who I had, in my infinite wisdom, written off.

I learned. I learned how a boy of ten could become the head of a household of five. How he became responsible for getting his brothers and sisters ready for school each morning. How he worried about how many cans of food were in the cabinet or, in his case, not in the cabinet. I learned how his mother had become so sick that he was sure that any day would be the end, especially without the surgery they could not afford. I learned about his father who was in jail and the weight of the world that was resting on the shoulders of this young, spirited boy. And here I was, angry over homework not being complete.

I became a different kind of teacher instantaneously. There was a war being fought against the social indifference to these children of the ghetto. The "hoodrats" with their saggy jeans and giant shirts buttoned at the top. The shaved heads and machismo bravado that permeated even the kindergarten. They were the throw away kids; they were the kids who took up space until they were caught tagging or worse and put into the penal system where they supposedly belonged. I was to become a soldier in this war—no, an officer. As an educator, I could take the fight back to those comfortable living rooms, with their large flat screen televisions and sophisticated libraries. I could shake up the worlds of those around me who were not in the trenches with me.

After Jose and I became a team against his hardship, we learned from each other. And, in a world where favorites are discouraged and fairness is the rule, he truly became one of my favorite human beings, for his heart, his strengths and weaknesses.

So, at the end of the year, when that decrepit bunny appeared on my desk, as if out of a magician's hat, I was moved to tears to find Jose behind the gesture. The bunny was a survivor, just like Jose. It was an artifact from a time of innocence, perhaps his last, when all he worried about was milk, sleep, and a clean diaper.

And when he asked if I liked the gift, I replied, "No. I love it."

Janin Spoor received a B.F.A. in acting from Otterbein College in Westerville, Ohio. After several years of waiting tables, she decided to pursue a different career path and got her teaching credential. She came to the classroom reluctantly but found a home. What she thought would be a short foray into education has become a career that has now spanned twelve years. She started teaching fifth grade but jumped at the chance to open a new school and teach sixth grade English and history. Recently, she moved to Hale Charter Academy where she currently teaches. Janin spent the summer of 2011 with the Cal State Northridge Writing Project's Invitational Summer Institute, where she "remembered" that writing was a source of great joy in her life. This is where she wrote "Some Bunny Loves You," which is her first publication.

Desperation

Tracey Kovar

"I want to kill myself...I am not sad. I am not mad. I am not happy. I am not angry. I am nothing." He said these words in a very straightforward, honest way, especially for an eight-year-old. We were sitting in a room alone. He had just returned from therapy, and my heart broke for him.

When I decided to write this, I tried to think of one word that could describe my past year of teaching. The word I came up with was desperation.

I am a special education teacher in an "at-risk" school. At the beginning of my last school year, eight of the first eleven shootings of the year happened within blocks of my school. Educators and non-educators alike often ask why I teach where I teach and if I am afraid to go to work every day. They ask if my husband is afraid for me to go to work.

I am not afraid. The only reason I can think of to explain my lack of "fear" is that I truly feel that I am where I am supposed to be. Besides, I get to come home every night to my nice house with my intact family in our lovely middle class neighborhood. I get to return home and put their reality behind me. I am blessed; I can return to the light of "my world" at the end of each day. For many of my students, school is their light; school is as good as it gets.

As a special education teacher in this setting, I often struggle with the question: "What is my role? Am I to educate these children? Am I to nurture these children?" Many educators realize a certain amount of nurturing and comforting needs to take place with many children before the learning can ever begin. However, many of my students' needs seem insurmountable. I go to work every day knowing I will face issues that may have no solution. I work with students who have all the cards stacked against them: economically, socially, environmentally and academically. I know the students I work with are desperate to survive. I also know when I go to work each day that if I am to attempt to meet the needs of my students, I first have to earn their trust. I have to prove myself to be an adult that is "in this with them" for the duration. They have to believe that I care; in order for me to meet their needs they have to believe in me. This is a difficult trust to establish with kids that have learned to trust no one.

***

"Mrs. K, my mom just got a new car, a pink Chevy. It's so fast the cops won't be able to catch her anymore." We were sitting in small group first thing in the morning. He said this with such pride; he was 7.

Economically, my students suffer from poverty. I see many students who are not clothed properly for the seasons or who wear clothing that is too small or too large. The majority of my students are on free or reduced breakfast and lunch. For many of them, these are the only two meals they receive in a day. Once, I worked in a middle/upper class private school. I had a prize box filled with trinkets; the students loved them. When I started at my current school, I pulled out my prize box with the trinkets, and my students were not all that interested. I asked my students what they would like to see in my prize box. They wanted some pretty typical items: crayons, markers, colored pens. But, they also wanted items students had never requested: hats, gloves, t-shirts and food.

***

I asked my class the question: "What would you do if you were the President?" The five fifth-graders in my writing group all responded with the same answer. "I would get rid of guns." They were eleven, and all of them knew someone who had been injured or killed due to gun violence.

Socially, my students suffer from their interaction with peers. I have noticed the pressure put on my male and female students not to show physical or emotional weakness. If weakness is shown, it is preyed upon ruthlessly. The behavior reminds me of nature and the "survival of the fittest." My students are very physical and very passionate in both joy and anger. It is as if there is a heightened energy surrounding the environment; you can almost physically feel it. This heightened energy can become explosive rather quickly, and I have learned some of the warning signs and how to redirect many situations to avoid confrontation.

***

"My dad took my mom out last night," he said.
"Where did he take her?" I asked.
"No," he replied. "He took her out, and she is in the hospital now."
It was nine in the morning, and we had just sat down for reading group. The boy was seven-years-old. He cried, and, inside, I cried for him.

Environmentally, my students suffer in their own families and neighborhoods. Few of my students live with intact families. The majority live in single parent households if they are lucky, others are with extended family or placed in foster care. After their school day, many of my students go home to empty houses. Their parents may be working or they simply are not home. The pressures my students endure in their neighborhood to be strong and to be in gangs are intense. A few of my students have parents that encourage this path. After all, gangs are what they did; it is what they know. Some see gangs as a means of survival.

***

"But, Mrs. K, I can't read." he yelled. We were seated in front of a computer and I had just read him the directions to the state reading test. I had explained to my nine-year-old student with autism, a non-reader, that he had to read the passages for this test. I could only help him read the questions.

Academically, my students struggle with learning disabilities, behavior disorders, and other health impairments. This combined with the aforementioned environmental challenges makes "getting an education" seem impossible to them. Some of my students come to school without the medication they need in order to function in a normal classroom setting. Others suffer from anxiety, low self-esteem and behavioral challenges, making it difficult for them to face their daily academic tasks and move ahead. Every day, I have to push my students, ask them to shelve their problems, and tell them move forward. What I am asking of them, many adults cannot even do. However, putting their problems aside for the day is an expectation I must have in order for them to succeed.

The desperation I see is not only among the students I work with every day. Many of my colleagues are desperate as well, desperate to make a connection, desperate to make a difference. We are hoping our students will understand what we are offering them: a different way of life through education. Many of my students struggle with this idea because they come from generations that have not valued education or that have been intimidated by education. I have to ask myself: How do you make a child understand what we are offering if their families don't value or understand what we are offering? How do you make a child understand the value of their education when they need to survive today? For many of them, the education road is too long and too difficult with too many obstacles in the way.

I will continue to go teach every day, side by side with my colleagues and we will continue to feel desperate, desperate to improve the lives of the students we work with each day.

Tracey Kovar received her B.S. in education and special education from the University of Nebraska—Omaha. After receiving her teaching credentials, she worked as a curriculum facilitator in Omaha, Nebraska. She took some time off from teaching to be a stay at home mom for her three children. When Tracey returned to teaching, she decided to take a position as a special education teacher. She works with students with special needs in kindergarten and first, second, third and sixth grades. She is currently working on her M.A. in curriculum and instruction from Concordia University in Seward, Nebraska. Tracey lives in Omaha with her wonderful husband, Kyle, and their three children.

Dreams of Prison

Jonathan Putman

"Sometimes I wish I could go to jail," he said.

He'd been pacing around the room since he started talking about himself. Not making much eye contact, pausing only briefly to poke at a paper on a desk or erase a letter on the board with his finger.

"You wanna know the truth about me?" he asked shortly after entering the classroom. It was only the two of us, and I hadn't asked him any questions.

"Only if you want to tell me," I said.

I hadn't known him very long. He was one of those students that show up on the roster sometime in March. One day, he was just there. Claimed he had done all of the work at his old school, read all the novels, knew all the skills. Of course, he couldn't tell me anything about the books he had read, had poor writing, refused to read aloud, didn't say much at all. Blended in.

"I came from Alabama, you know."

"You told me that, yeah. Do you miss it?" I asked.

"The truth?" Again with this word "truth." I got the sense he was not used to telling the truth, not about himself at least.

"My mother died of an overdose. Cocaine. I was eight." The pacing started. "Had to move in with my aunty and her husband. Man used to abuse me and my sisters." He stopped for a second to open the cover of a dictionary, let it drop closed and continued. "I shoulda killed that man. When I turned eighteen, I came up here or else I was gonna kill that man. I shoulda done it, too. I remember watchin' him beat my little sisters." His words trailed off.

I had just submitted his final grade the day before. It was a D. Easily could have been an F. He had done some of the work. Some of it he had even tried hard to do well on. The points said D, but just looking at the standards, it was an F.

"My father was in jail most of my life. When I heard he got out, I tol' him I was comin up here. Man it's hard. Stupid recession. Can't find no work. My father's a ex-con, ain't no one gonna hire him," he said. "That's why you lookin for me, you find me on the corners, that's where I be."

"What do you want to do with your life?" I asked.

"Navy. My grandfather was in the army. He left me money, but that man down in Alabama took it. He didn't want me to come up here."

"Why not?"

"Power thing, I guess. He wanted power. I shoulda done it."

"So, what about the Navy? Have you talked to a recruiter?" I said trying to shift him back to his future.

"Not enough credits. I either gotta do summer school or come back next year, and I don't think I can make it that long."

A couple of weeks earlier I had the students write poems about what success meant to them. He wrote a poem titled, "The 5 Stars 2 Success." His 5 "stars" were confidence, motivation, goals, determination, and power. I tried to refer to those in an attempt to switch the mood of the conversation.

"Remember your poem," I said, pointing to where it hung of the bulletin board. "Remember what you wrote, 'enduring the hardships and adversity life brings and staying focused no matter what.'"

"You white guys are funny, man," he said with a big grin. The first smile since he had come in. "You cool. I had a real good friend back home. My boy. We grew up together. He was white. You guys are cool. Funny, man." His pacing started up again. His eyes showed that he was going back again. Back to Alabama. My attempt to get him to look forward had failed.

"It's different down there, you know."

"How?"

"Safer. You could walk the streets all night long and not get shot. I lived in big ol' house down there too."

"Sounds like you're better off up here though, right?"

"Maybe." He paused for a long time. "I've never felt so...I don't know. Hopeless."

There is a sign that hangs in our hallway, "Every Student College Bound." What about this student? As we moved toward an emphasis on college, we got rid of all the trade programs in school. I remember my high school had a working photo lab, a drafting program, and a full auto shop. There was a senior career semester where the school would help students find jobs. We could earn credits while getting paid. There was even a whole semester of construction. Students would spend the semester building a house from the ground up and sell it at the end of the year. The school I'm at now has one career program: culinary arts. I hear they are cutting the program next year.

"Sometimes I wish I could go to jail," he said.

"Say that again," I replied.

"At least it would get me off the streets," he said while awkwardly picking at the corner of a poster on the wall.

"Look," I said, "is there anyone you want to talk to?"

"I'm talkin to you."

"I mean a counselor, or a…"

"Naw." He cut me off. "They can't do nothin'. I prefer talkin' to you. You cool."

"Well look," I said, "if there's anything I can do…"

"I appreciate it," again cutting me off. "I'll be alright. I'll figure it out. Thanks." He stepped out into the hall. Blended in.

Jonathan Putnam received a M.A.T. from National Louis University. He currently teaches English and drama on the west side of Chicago. Before entering the Chicago Public School system, Jonathan co-founded the multi-arts organization, Hermit Arts, where he served as an actor, director, writer, and producer. He has performed all over the United States and taught English in China and South Korea. He now resides in Chicago with his beautiful wife and son.

The Last Days of Marshall High

Mark Pomeroy

A week from graduation, she walks into her English class, sits down and looks to the overhead screen for the day's prompt—Neighborhood. For a minute, she quiets herself, pen in hand.

With each passing day, school seems both closer and more distant. Surges of memory. Her teachers, her classes these past four years, all the hallway conversations, the languages. The halls used to be more crowded, livelier, but now some of her classmates show up every other day, if that.

Her teachers tell them they matter, no one is abandoning them. They can't take it personally, that's the thing. Life's not always fair. And they know it's true, and also, enrollment was on the low side compared to other high schools.

Still. This place is theirs. For some kids, it's home, where they can come to know that people will pay attention to what they're thinking. Where they can find a few moments of calm. Where they can eat.

"I live in the wilderness of the economy," she writes on the first line of her paper.

***

He can't seem to stay awake.

When his math teacher asks him to step into the hallway, he stands slowly from his desk and pulls up his baggy pants.

"How much sleep did you get last night?" the man asks.

"I don't know. Four hours."

"You need between eight and 10. What did you eat for breakfast?"

"Nothing."

"Not hungry?"

"I don't know. A little."

The teacher hesitates, gauging him. "Let me know if you're not getting any breakfast, all right? If you need any help."

Face tingling, he avoids the man's eyes and gives a nod.

In the fall, he's supposed to begin his sophomore year at a new school in another neighborhood, one he's never been to, and the thought of that makes his stomach tighter.

***

She watches her students leave, waiting until the classroom goes quiet. Her eyes rest for a few beats on each place where a kid just sat, and calmly she begins to tell.

The father had an accident at work; they didn't have insurance. They lost their house. Alcoholic mother. Runaway. Father in jail. Homeless and living in a car.

Her voice remains steady, and when she finishes going around, an electric stillness fills the room.

"Yet here they are, in class," she says. "Writing."

***

The brick building stands. The surrounding grounds need mowing.

This place, in this far part of the forward-hurtling city—a high school drenched with decades of stories, this cornerstone of a neighborhood—awaits its fate.

Emptied of so much tenacious hope, it's finally silent.

Mark Pomeroy has received an Oregon Literary Fellowship for fiction, and his poems, stories, and essays have appeared in *Open Spaces Quarterly*, *The Oregonian*, *The Wordstock Ten*, and the *Waco Tribune-Herald*. A former classroom teacher, he holds an M.A. in English education from Teachers College, Columbia University. He lives with his family in Portland, Oregon, where he divides his time between working on a novel and teaching high school writing workshops through the Literary Arts Writers in the Schools program.

Teaching Means Creating Connections

Going Places

Susanne Rubenstein

He is hunkered down behind his copy of *The Glass Menagerie*. He wears an intense expression, one I have not seen him wear these many days we've spent with Tom, Laura, and a world of glass animals. I make my way to the back of the room and sidle up behind him. Just as I expected. He's not waltzing around the room with Laura; he's speeding down the highway.

"Josh," I say. "Put the driver's manual away."
He looks up sheepishly. Caught. He pulls the booklet out of the pages of the play.

"But, Ms. R.," he pleads, "I gotta pass this test."
I sympathize. In his sixteen-year-old mind, his future depends on it. What I wish, though, is that it were the only test he had to pass.

***

I teach in Massachusetts where, in order to ultimately obtain a high school diploma, tenth graders are required to pass a rigorous state examination, the Massachusetts Comprehensive Assessment System (MCAS). Given in grades three through eight and ten, the test has become a driving force behind English language arts curricula. And I, like teachers all across the nation, am discovering what it means to be "accountable" and to have to make certain that my students "measure up."

But this is a teachable moment. Josh is going on about the learner's permit test.

"There are so many rules! You have to know so much!" he moans.

Other students chime in. They talk about the dreaded road test. They speak of strict examiners, of seconds counted at stop signs, of hands positioned just so on the wheel.

I listen to them complain. "But it's worth it, isn't it?" I ask. "When you pass?"

They look at me as if I'm crazy. Of course it is, their expressions say.

Lisa tosses her head. "It's freedom, Ms. R.," she explains. "With a license, you can go places."

I nod. "With a diploma, you can too."

And then, before they can groan and give me that "not another teacher talk" look, I say, "Let me give you an analogy."

***

There is a comparison here. The driving test and the MCAS. Both are required by the state. Both involve preparation and training. Both, in a short amount of time, affect a long future. Both demand evidence of competence, skill, and an adult sensibility. And, if we are being honest, both ask students to perform in a way that they are unlikely to ever have to perform again.

They listen, acknowledging the parallels I draw. But, at last, they blink. This seems a sort of heresy. Is their teacher speaking up against the driving test . . . or the MCAS? Is she implying that these tests are worthless, groundless, even unfair?

I shake my head. "No," I tell them. "The tests serve an important purpose. For one, you must prove you know every rule of the road, and you must demonstrate your ability to navigate those roads in the safest fashion possible. For the other, you must prove you know the rules of language, and you must demonstrate your ability to put those rules to work in a clear, concise piece of writing. Both skills, safe driving and smooth writing, are necessary in the world, and so you have to pass the tests to..." I smile at Lisa, "go places. But . . ."

I pause and look around the classroom at those students who I know already hold that precious license. "How many of you drive a little differently now than you did on the day of your road test?"

They snicker. Rob says he's pushed his seat way back; he doesn't like sitting up straight. Andrea tells us that music is always blaring when she drives. And Peter confesses that he has sneaked through a few yellow lights.

"So here's what I'm saying," I tell them. "The fact is, neither the RMV examiner or the MCAS scorer is looking for you to be creative, to show your individual style on the pavement or on the paper.

What you need to prove in order to pass both these important tests—to hold a license or a diploma—is competence, a demonstration of adult ability and responsibility as required by the test.

"To pass your driving test, you keep two hands on the wheel in the proper position, and you count the number of seconds you sit at the stop sign. You keep the radio off and the seat up straight, and you prove to that person sitting beside you with the clipboard that you know how to drive. In the same way, on the day you take that MCAS Long Composition test, you study the prompt closely, and you write a solid thesis statement. You perfect your topic sentences, and you check and recheck every bit of your writing for errors. Then you send your work off to another person with a clipboard, who will make a final evaluation of your competence.

"And after—when you've passed?"

"Then," I say, "is when you take a long breath and recognize that the test is one thing and real life something else. That doesn't mean that you can stop sitting patiently at stop signs or that you can ever take your eyes off the road. But you can relax a little. You can turn the radio on and adjust your hands on the wheel and begin to develop a driving style that is your own, as long as you remember that you can never test the limits of safety. Likewise, with the MCAS behind you, you can write about what matters to you. You can experiment with style and subject, and you have time for reflection, response, and revision. You can put yourself on paper with an eye toward an audience you've chosen. But remember, when your writing is ready for publication, it has to be right, in content and conventions."

Twenty-six sophomores nod. They get it. They really do.

***

I'm not so sure that all teachers—or administrators—get it though, and that is what worries me these days. It seems that under the pressure that widespread testing, evaluations, and accountability bring, too many of us have forgotten who we are as English teachers. And so, like a mantra, I've come to repeat to myself these five words: I am a writing teacher. This means my goal is to teach my students to write— from their minds and from their hearts. I want them to own their words. I want each student to develop a unique voice and style. I want them to understand that writing is discovery, filled with extraordinary moments when the writer suddenly sees the world in a way he or she never has before. I want my students to struggle, sweat, and swear they cannot write one more word, only to experience the satisfaction that comes when that one elusive word or idea finds its way to the page. I want them to feel the intimate connection between author and audience, and I want them to write for the world, believing in the power of publication. And so I add to my mantra: I am a writing teacher, and my students are writers.

Am I abdicating my responsibility as an English teacher in 2011? Am I retreating to a simpler teaching time, ignoring that today we teach in an age of high standards and even higher stakes? No. I believe I am clear sighted and committed. I know that my students, like those all across the country, must pass challenging state assessments based on carefully constructed frameworks and standards. I accept that it is my responsibility to give my students the knowledge and skills necessary to be successful on such tests.

But I don't believe that my responsibility ends there. Of course, we owe our students the best chance possible to succeed on high stakes tests. But we owe them so much more than that. We owe them a sense of themselves as writers, and with that will come the capacity for critical thought, creativity, and clear communication. With that, too, will come an appreciation of writing as art.

That is one more thing that we as English teachers need to remember. Writing is an art, and a test can only measure a skill. Though as teachers we are loath to admit it. The truth is that it is entirely possible for a student to write a vacuous, voiceless essay on a state mandated test and score well. Although that essay may be devoid of voice and style, it can still show mastery of form and organization as well as proficiency with mechanics. It can meet the standards of the test rubric and yet seem curiously flat. As such, it is a striking product of writing instruction gone wrong and of a student writer who has learned the lesson of such test-focused instruction too well: do what is expected, abide by the conventions, and, above all, do not take a risk. And that, sadly, becomes the definition of writing.

So we as teachers, many of us long committed to teaching writing as an art, find ourselves caught in a dilemma, discovering that what we've always fostered in the classroom may not be what state assessments measure. The high stakes tests my students face are not designed to assess long-term writing growth or the development of style, voice, and creative expression. Rather these tests are intended to measure what they can measure—primarily a student's ability to produce timed writing that shows evidence of organization and skills-based learning. That is a reality, one that other teachers and I have to live with.

But we do not have to sacrifice our principles—or our students—in order to live peaceably and productively with this reality. We can give our students the means and methods to succeed on standardized tests by teaching test writing as a unique and legitimate genre with its own particular style and audience, not much different from a road test. And, after that, we can give our students license to sit back and enjoy the ride and the exhilaration that writing—writing from the heart—can bring.

***

Josh has found his place in *The Glass Menagerie*. "Tom writes poems in the bathroom? At work?" He looks at me quizzically. I nod and survey the room. "Any ideas why?"

"He hates his job?"

"He likes poems?"

"He loves the bathroom?" There's laughter. Then, from the corner, a voice.

"He can't go anywhere. He's stuck at home and at the warehouse. His poems take him places."

There is silence. I look at Lisa. She cocks her head and gives me a small smile. We all sit in the stillness of her wisdom and in the mystery that connects all things. I don't have to say a word. But, if I did, here is what I would say.

Writing does take you places, just as surely as does your father's Subaru or a merchant sailor's ship. Writing takes you down paths as curvy and confusing as the most backwoods country lanes or as speedy and straightforward as the widest expanse of sea.

Writing lets you travel roads you've never before tested, and the discoveries you make along the way can leave you breathless.

Writing is always an adventure. There will be dead ends and dead calms and moments when it seems you're very lost, but always around another corner will be something new, something you never before imagined.

There are those who will tell you to chart your route carefully, to prepare and pack well, to leave nothing to chance. But I disagree. The most exciting journeys are those you take without a map.

I continue to hope that teachers will encourage their students to take a wild and daring journey. It is a journey that is neither straightforward nor safe nor solitary. It is the journey from student to writer, and, though there is something of a route defined by the process necessary to produce strong writing, all the stages of the journey—prewriting, drafting, sharing, responding, rewriting, editing and publishing—are entangled and entwined. And so each young traveler must forge his own best path.

I hope, too, that teachers will find the courage to take their own journey. For veteran teachers, it may be a journey back to a time when we felt less the pressures of accountability, when we trusted more to our own experience and expertise, and when we still believed there is a touch of mystery to writing well. For new teachers, many themselves products of a society that has measured their ability via a test, it may be a journey to a new land where success cannot always be always be quantified, but it can be recognized and rewarded. For all of us, it can be a journey of extraordinary discovery.

***

The class is almost over. Amid the rustle of papers and rumble of voices, I hear Josh.

"So why does Tom give in? Why doesn't he fight for what he wants?"

"He does." It's Lisa again, and it's clear that she has read ahead. I give her a look that says, "Don't spoil the ending for them," and she sighs. With great restraint, she settles for, "It isn't easy, you know." And I think, how right you are.

The bell sounds, and they are up and headed for the door. Josh tosses the driver's manual into the air and catches it deftly. He gives me a thumbs up.

"No sweat, " he says.

I smile. Confidence, I think, that's half the battle for all of us. I watch his back, as he goes out the door. He's going places.

Susanne Rubenstein teaches English at Wachusett Regional High School in Holden, Massachusetts. She is the author of *Raymond Carver in the Classroom: "A Small, Good Thing"* (NCTE 2005) and *Go Public! Encouraging Student Writers to Publish* (NCTE 1998). Her fiction and poetry have appeared in such publications as *Literal Latte, The MacGuffin* and *The Worcester Review*. Her essays on teaching have been published in *The Christian Science Monitor, Voices from the Middle, School Arts*, and *Teacher Magazine* as well as a number of collections, including NCTE's *Short Stories in the Classroom*. Susanne is a consultant for the National Council of Teachers of English Professional Development Network and frequently presents workshops on writing and contemporary literature for teachers and students. She is also involved in working with pre-service teachers.

Normal Folks Need Not Apply

Jennifer W. Anderson

I've heard it numerous times, "I wouldn't teach middle school for all the money in the world! They're nothing but a bunch of smart-alecks." Yeah, well it takes one to teach one, if you know what I mean.

You have to be a little off your rocker to teach in a middle school, no doubt. I knew this from personal experience. Yet I didn't realize how universal this was until last year. Our school board spent money on professional development that actually was beneficial to the math and science teachers. Instead of forcing us to sit through a lecture about how to use a required program, which we would half-heartedly use, they hired a consultant. This consultant had been in an actual classroom of her own, had spent lots of time in others' classrooms, and had a lot to share. But, most importantly, she knew how to run a workshop. She took the time to allow us to share our ideas with each other and allowed us to lead the agenda. We learned a lot from each other this year.

Middle school math teachers from across the parish ("county" for you non-Louisianans) gathered every month or two with the consultant. She would model ideas from our classrooms and others across the country, and we would share our worries, stories, and teaching strategies. Sure, we learned about learning stations, effectively using the textbook, and how to teach vocabulary. But the one thing that stuck with me is how much imagery we use in our classrooms.

If you want grab the attention of tweens, especially in a potentially dry subject like math, you have to be willing to be silly or even act like an out-right idiot. Using imagery is a way to accomplish this. Imagery is not a subject to be left in the English/language arts classroom. It's necessary for those students who are not natural number manipulators. For instance, you may hear me say, "We love Dolly Parton, but we don't love Dolly Parton fractions." Like my students, you may be asking, "What's a Dolly Parton fraction?" Well, they are the ones that are heavy on top, the improper ones. If students don't catch the imagery, I just feign innocence with a wink, "You know…she has such big hair."

Speaking of simplifying improper fractions or changing fractions to decimals, kids can't seem to remember which number is the divisor and which is the dividend. Well, in this case, they can see the fraction as a cowboy (numerator) riding a horse (denominator). When the cowboy gets thirsty, he goes into the house (the division bracket, which has an even more ridiculously technical term) and the horse stays outside. Now you can divide and get a decimal, not a whole number.

I teach in a laboratory school, and I share a very large space divided by a mere row of bookshelves. This means my "roommate," as I call the math teacher next door, and I can hear each other teaching. She always chuckles at my use of the term "naked number." I don't want to see naked numbers, especially in geometry, where we use units. If the answer is "15 cm," you'll better not give me a naked "15." The teacher next door isn't laughing at my use of imagery, she's really laughing at how I draw the word out in my most Southern way. Apparently, in my room, it's a naaaaaked number. (By the way, I stole that cowboy and horse image from her.)

Education students frequent my classroom, and they just never know what they'll hear. This past year, we were reviewing multiplying and dividing integers. Those rules are difficult for students to remember for some reason. To me, they are simple: same sign means the answer is positive, different signs mean the answer is negative. A student, who had a transferred from a local school, taught me a different way. "A pretty person and a pretty person make a pretty baby. An ugly person and an ugly person make a pretty baby. But an ugly person and a pretty person make an ugly baby," he announced one afternoon as a row of observers looked at him in shock. I quickly told them that he had come from another school. I told his former teacher this story during one of our workshops, and we got a good laugh over it. I'm considering using it next year, though. This summer, I am tutoring a young lady from another school. She struggled with all those rules and procedures her teacher used, but she's starting to get it using the imagery I use.

Since some of the better math teachers are willing to go out on a limb and be silly in class, I would like to give some advice to principals looking for math teachers willing to do anything, including looking like an idiot, in order for students to learn. Be sure to include in your recruiting advertisement, "Normal folks need not apply."

Jennifer Wilbanks Anderson is a middle school teacher at Northwestern State University (N.S.U.) Middle Lab School in Louisiana. She currently teaches math but is also certified in English/language arts and social studies. Jennifer decided to teach middle school after she taught journalism at N.S.U. for five years and worked for a local radio station. She missed teaching, so she enrolled in N.S.U.'s PREP Program to obtain alternative certification. Jennifer is a teacher consultant with the N.S.U. Writing Project, an affiliate of the National Writing Project. In this role, she hosts workshops on how to use iPads and iPod Touch with literacy strategies and workshops on writing to learn in the math curriculum. She has also led workshops in engagement strategies and protocols for discuss to improve school quality. Jennifer lives in Natchitoches, Louisiana. She is married to Garrett and has the cutest kids in the parish, Katie and Sawyer.

Teaching To Kill A Mockingbird

Kelly Norris

"Oh my God. What's that?"

The other teacher with me looked as though she'd found a mutilated animal on her front doorstep. Scrawled across my white board in lopsided red letters was:

Fuck you Mrs N
Nigger lover

"I don't know," I muttered, frozen. We had just returned to school from the long Martin Luther King weekend. My stomach tightened, as I panicked. Was someone after me? Who did this? Where were they right now? I started picturing all of my students, but, as their faces flew by, I just felt more and more in the dark; it could have been any one of them. Or, was it an adult? A parent? A janitor? Another teacher?

"Let me get someone," my colleague suggested, and she disappeared. Five minutes later, when the administrators arrived, I was still standing in the same spot.

***

I had been teaching in Wilbraham since the fall. It was my first and only interview at a high school in Western Massachusetts, and I accepted the job the day of the interview. It was a school in the suburbs, right on the edge of Springfield, the area's most underserved city. The community was almost all white with a small population of students of color who mostly came from Springfield through school choice programs. Standing in front of the board now, my mind went back to a conversation I had had with my freshman class about race. We had been reading the assigned text for the course, *To Kill a Mockingbird*, which contained the phrase that glared at me from the board that morning; this time not directed at the main character, Atticus, but at me. I had told the class I didn't feel comfortable saying the word "nigger" aloud and said, "n-word" instead, but we hadn't discussed the issue much more than that.

The class was entirely white. One of the kids, Jake, had talked about avoiding seeing a movie in Springfield because he was afraid he might get shot. I had commented that that was not a realistic view. Running over this and other conversations in my mind, I searched for a hint about something incendiary I might have said or who may have been silently in a rage all that time. Could it have been Jake, who was just doing a great job of covering it up? It frightened me that I didn't have a clue. Meanwhile, a cop and the administrators of the school had gathered around the board and were discussing the subtleties of the handwriting. An all-out hunt for the perpetrator was on, and I was subsequently ignored.

Even after this shattering experience, my trials with *To Kill A Mockingbird* were not over. The following year, Raymond, a black student from Springfield stormed out of my room, upset by the novel. "This book is racist!" he shouted and headed out the door. I didn't blame him for wanting to leave. Here was a portrayal of white, racist characters in a room full of white students with a white teacher and little to no discussion of how we were to handle this content. Wanting to find a way to teach this book that would be a positive, empowering experience for Raymond as well as Jake, I realized I had to learn to navigate the inflammatory territory of race and racism. And I had to learn fast because the book was required for every freshman English class.

***

Learning to teach about racism went hand-in-hand with confronting my own understandings and experiences of race. The first book I picked up was Beverly Tatum's *Why Are All the Black Kids Sitting Together in the Cafeteria?* I was introduced to the concept of race as "a system of advantage" that benefited whites. This led me to pick up another book explicitly addressing white privilege: Tim Wise's *White Like Me*. It was scary to confront my own internalized biases and assumptions, but I plowed through, determined to make myself a better teacher, which ultimately began by being a better person. I wrote my personal narrative based on race and shared those experiences with others at a conference focused on the concept of white privilege

Conference. All of this personal transformation happened as I continued teaching the book. As I went, I tried to share parts of my process with the students.

I began by tentatively reading to the class an excerpt from the internet on the history of the "n-word." This brief lesson set the tone for open but serious conversations about race. It gave us the language to begin talking. Students asked me, "When should I use 'black' and when should I use 'person of color'?" Without pretending to have all the answers, I discussed these questions with them, and we investigated the history of the language. I was careful never to call on a student of color in the room to provide answers for us and even to correct the white students who would frequently do so. Instead, I went on-line, ordered books, read articles, and talked to anyone who would listen.

The next year I coupled this background writing on the "n-word" with the poem "The Incident" by Countee Cullen. We discussed the impact of racism, in particular the "n-word." I stopped short of having students journal on their personal experiences of discrimination or prejudice, but, the next year, we added this step. At the suggestion of a friend, I went to a website on anti-racism[8] and found more probing journal prompts the next year such as:

> *What is your background (race, ethnicity, gender, socio-economic class, religion, etc.)? What is one thing that is good about growing up with these social identities? What is one thing that is difficult about growing up with these social identities? And, What is the earliest time in your life that you can remember being aware that there were people in the world whose skin was a different color than yours? What thoughts and feelings to you have about that memory and what happened then?*

We paired up to share answers and then had whole class discussions where students took steps out of their comfort zones to ask hard questions and make confessions. White students shared about being told not to play with black neighbors and black students shared about being followed in the store. I learned to know when to back off, when to allow silence to happen and how to return to issues later, once I was more informed. Most importantly, I learned I didn't have to know it all in order to begin, I just had to take a leap and start somewhere.

***

Soon, this small opening unit found its way into a pre-reading research project. Carefully selecting groups, I assigned topics to give historical background to the book. One group made a timeline of African-American history, one studied the case of the Scottsboro Boys, another learned about white anti-racists and another, black anti-racists. As I learned more about these topics alongside the students in our school's media center, I found myself engaged in rigorous conversations with small groups or individual students. These more focused discussions were powerful; I could challenge students to explore their own views, like the student who told me "Black students going to lower achieving schools isn't racism; it's just how it is; it's just a fact." I responded with a question: "But why is that how it is? Is that fair?" She scowled at me, reddened and walked away. I quickly learned I had to support students through this material as well. I made sure to seek her out later. "This stuff is hard," I said. "But it's important to think about. Don't give up." Too much challenge, I learned, caused students to shut down or even act out. But too much support could turn into validation for their biases. It was a line of balance I grew more and more familiar with.

At a staff training session on diversity and anti-racism (the school continued having incidents of racially motivated attacks), we were introduced to the PBS documentary, *Race: The Power of an Illusion*, which documented the absence of biological racial categories and the history of how and why racism developed. Inspired by my new understandings, I added another pre-reading research group to explore the history of race and racism and directed them to the website for the documentary. This hand-picked group also studied different meanings for the term racism including Tatum's "system of advantage" and Peggy McIntosh's concept of "white privilege." I worked closely with them, sharing my own steps to understanding and helping them sift out what was most accessible. They also needed my support planning their presentation; just because they could grasp the difficult concepts did not mean it would be easy presenting it to their peers.

***

Finally, when we began the journey into the book, all of this background knowledge allowed us to discuss it critically in terms of its historical accuracy and its presentation of race, racism, and anti-racism. We discussed how effective Atticus was as an anti-racist leader and how Harper Lee's background influenced her depiction of black characters. Students identified the unrealistic absence of a black response to the racism enacted against Tom Robinson and the value judgment placed on "standard English" in comparison to "African-American English." Meanwhile, we continued through writing and talking to share personal stories about ourselves and our identities on a regular basis, in what became a safe yet stimulating classroom environment.

***

What began as a traumatic experience has become one of the units I now most look forward to teaching. I learned that support is out there for dealing with racially loaded content and that we as teachers have a responsibility to go through the discomfort of learning about race and racism ourselves if we are to teach it. What I hope to challenge myself and my students with next is an outreach project where we identify lingering effects of racism in our community and take steps to interrupt it. The possibilities presented by *To Kill A Mockingbird* are endless as long you can accept its provocative nature as an invitation to growth, for you and your students.

Kelly Norris received a B.A. in comparative literature from the University of Massachusetts and an M.A. in education from the University of Bridgeport in Connecticut. She has taught high school English in Boston and Bridgeport and currently teaches in Wilbraham, Massachusetts. Along with teaching, she is the founding advisor of an after-school club supporting students of color in her district and is a member of a Western Massachusetts chapter of Alliance of White Anti-Racists (AWAR). Her essays have been published in *The Pressures of Teaching* published by Kaplan and the on-line journal *Critical Education*. She is currently seeking publication of a memoir about a year abroad in West Africa. Kelly lives with her husband and daughter in Western Massachusetts.

Halloween Lessons

Danielle Hall

Halloween and Valentine's Day are the high holy days in an elementary school classroom. Whatever their original intent, these days are now about the pleasure of being ten years old. My enthusiasm for these holidays was born out of inexperience: at twenty-two, I had never hosted a class party. The previous winter, I impulsively left the East Coast to start teaching third grade on the eastern edge of the Navajo Reservation in New Mexico. I was a bright-eyed and inexperienced art major hired on an emergency waiver in January; my students considered me a dubious prospect.

Despite my students' initial declarations that they were "the worst kids in the school" and that I "won't last 'til March," I survived to summer vacation. When the fourth grade teacher threatened to quit after meeting my students on step-up day, I was permitted to follow my class to the next grade. The principal even offered me a "portable," a double-wide trailer serving as an exterior classroom. We both pretended this was a generous offer.

With a fresh start in the fall, my students and I got through the opening month of school with only two write-ups for insubordination (me), and one fire-extinguisher related trip to the emergency room (my student Luke). We all agreed that this was cause for celebration. School board policy, however, dictated no more than two parties per year. My students informed me there were five different holidays that warranted a party, including "sheep butchering day" in the spring. Celebrating each special event surely would draw my principal's ire, yet I was unwilling to pass up my first Halloween party.

Unsure how to proceed, I visited our third grade teacher, Barb. A veteran educator of some forty years, she brightened when I asked for advice. "I have some Halloween-themed word scrambles," she offered. When I asked about a party, she shook her head incredulously. "We'll find you locked in a closet somewhere. The kids will be halfway to town by the time we get you out."

I left her room despondent. Surely there was option other than a day of worksheets or an out-of-control party. Mulling over the possibilities, I remembered an article I read about project-based learning. Within this methodology, students learned a variety of skills and concepts while carrying out a real world endeavor. What if I used project-based learning to set up an authentic, student-designed Halloween project? My eyes grew wide; we could create a haunted house for the school!

I called my father, a high school teacher, to share my great idea.

His lack of enthusiasm was clear through the long distance connection. "The complexity of these projects are challenging even for experienced teachers. Without outstanding behavior management," he paused, cleared his throat, "your classroom could descend into chaos."

"That won't be a problem," I replied breezily. "They're really excited about the topic!" I started sketched haunted house plans, his final words lost as I crunched the phone against my shoulder. "Uh huh, right. Thanks for the advice, Dad!" I hung up elated. This was the best idea ever.

***

Even with my naive exuberance, I realized my wolf pack of fourth graders needed help to carry out an elaborate and time-consuming project. I enlisted the support of Cheryl, our unwaveringly optimistic fifth grade teacher. She had a class of over thirty students, few of whom spoke English fluently, and her classroom assistant's main skill was smiling handsomely. I reasoned Cheryl could use a celebration, even one disguised as a learning experience. She wholeheartedly agreed.

Over the next several evenings, Cheryl and I diligently prepared to share our proposal with the principal. When we arrived at our appointed meeting time, however, the office was in an uproar. One of the two school buses had a flat tire on the long afternoon route. Our principal, clutching a phone in one hand and a parent telephone list in the other, gave us an inattentive nod of approval. It was official: fourth and fifth graders would host a haunted house and Halloween crafts for the entire school.

I broke the news to my class the first week of October. A moment of big, swiveling stares to their friends. "Really?" Luke asked incredulously. His hair had just begun to grow in, hiding the ridge of staples across his scalp. "You mean we're going to turn our classroom into a giant haunted house for the whole school?"

Devon got the real message. "You mean we get to scare little kids and make them cry? Alright!"

I had forgotten how many fifth grade students were in one classroom. It was hard to maneuver around desks, and children seemed to be talking everywhere. My fourth graders tucked themselves into the far perimeter of the room, unusually silent. We, the adults in the room, focused our introductory conversation on the big picture of the student-centered project. The fourth grade classroom would be the haunted house; the fifth grade classroom would have scary story readings and Halloween craft projects. Teams of students would organize and host each part of the event, from tour guides to make-up artists. We were thoughtful in assessing the needs of our students, and considered appropriate developmental tasks to enhance their collaboration skills in a real life environment. But we were suddenly drowned by ten, eleven, twelve year olds shouting. Cheryl and I shrugged, trusting this was just first day excitement. They would settle down when we started the academic components. Right?

***

Our first day of authentic, child-centered project learning: children wandered around with handfuls of plastic spiders and orange crepe paper, asking what they were supposed to be doing. I waded through the room, trying to encourage different groups to complete basic tasks. "How are the posters coming?" I asked our publicity group.

Devon was drawing a picture of a dwarf with his head cut off. He paused long enough to look up at me, his face smooth in confusion. "We're supposed to make posters? Oh. Huh... Do you like the blood coming out of the dwarf's neck?"

A week passed, and my classroom was a battlefield for pumpkins and ghosts. Every inch of carpet was covered with butcher paper: orange, black, red, blue paper was rolled and swarmed by artists. Paint spilled several times, glopping in the reading area with a pasty damp smell. Two fourth graders decided to color themselves in chalk. I found myself leaping over murals of flying black cats to catch them, white and yellow dust rising in the air like smoke. I made a brief check out the window and saw two students running around the playground in costumes, chasing each other with sticks. Realizing something might be awry in the fifth grade classroom, I herded my group back into the school building as fast as I could move them.

We opened the heavy metal classroom door to see masses of children in costumes and masks. Several boys raced by us, chasing each other with plastic swords. In the far corner, a cluster of girls shrieked as they pulled on different wigs. It seemed the entire group of students was shouting, fighting, leaping over desks. Cheryl was nowhere to be found, but in the center of the room stood the fifth grade assistant, Lowell. He laughed as he handed a devil's costume to a boy. "This suits you," he gibed.

The blood drained out of my face. "Lowell? LOWELL?!" My voice was shrill over the din.

The aide turned with a face as wide and innocent as my students'. "Yeah?" Kids continued to fling themselves around the classroom in the background. "What?"

The next morning, my principal requested a meeting. Children running wild on the playground tipped him off that something was awry. "What, *precisely*, are your students learning?" He stared over his glasses, fingertips pressed under his chin. I explained they were developing essential leadership skills while studying the history and folklore of American culture. I didn't mention I feared we wouldn't finish in time, or that I didn't know if my students were truly learning when they drew pictures of ghosts for haunted house decorations.

"Everything correlates to educational objectives," I said instead, gesturing to my thick book of New Mexico learning standards. "So we're all set?"

No, we were not all set. My principal informed me that since he gave us initial—albeit inattentive—approval of the Halloween learning project, he couldn't cancel the event. However, he sternly insisted that teachers participating in our Halloween celebration submit lesson plans for the event that clearly demonstrated alignment with state standards. Anyone who failed to do so would be written up for insubordination.

"I have grave concerns about the educational value of this event," he said as he walked me to the door. "It would be best to abandon it."

I nodded, attempting to look obedient. Inside, my heart was

shaking. How could we cancel the event now? Our students were so excited. They would cry or, more likely, rise up in a Halloween-themed rebellion. I would end up locked in the closet after all.

Stubbornly determined to see this through, I started a secret campaign. I snuck into each classroom at lunch with a list of Halloween related, grade level appropriate standards. By the end of the week, every teacher submitted a Halloween celebration lesson plan to our principal. *Your move*, I secretly dared him.

***

Halloween day finally dawned. My students arrived in all variations of costumes. The cafeteria vibrated during breakfast with the excitement. Fourth and fifth graders bounced between loudly bragging about the coolness of their plans to turning a little white with fear at the approaching activities. Their excitement was interrupted by our principal reading morning announcements over the loudspeaker.

"Good morning, students. We, per school board policy, must have a bomb drill. Today. Most likely it would be in the afternoon, regrettably, at the same time as the Halloween festivities. In addition," he intoned, "Any classroom teacher that does not demonstrate prompt, orderly evacuations will be written up for violating school board policy."

I blanched. How was I going to evacuate a haunted house full of children? I looked around the cafeteria. Even the teachers were in costume; one painted his chest green as the Incredible Hulk. We couldn't cancel now. In the hectic minutes before the Pledge of Allegiance, Cheryl and I frantically crafted a haunted house bomb drill evacuation plan. Somehow, we would see this through.

In spite of the high, wild energy saturating the school, we made it through morning lessons. I skipped lunch to mix up fake blood from corn syrup and food coloring for Jesus, who planned to dramatically gulp it from a plastic cup during the haunted house. I spent the remaining recess turning my Navajo students into the scariest creatures they could imagine: dead *biliganas* (white people).

For the first time I could remember, parents appeared at school. They quietly slipped in the classroom, wearing costumes and carrying treats. I asked Cheryl if she sent home letters to families about the event. She shook her head no, then slid away to introduce herself to a father. We had never met most of these parents. Our students' families were notoriously wary of school due to the painful and oppressive legacy of Bureau of Indian Affairs boarding schools. These schools, now defunct, harshly punished young students for celebrating their cultural traditions. Many grandparents, and some parents, had attended these schools as children. They were left with an inherent distrust of educational systems. Consequentially, most avoided school events.

I tentatively approached Mrs. Begaye, our home-school liaison. She was the hawk-like matriarch of our surrounding community. "Do you know why parents came today?" I asked softly.

She looked at me levelly. "They wanted to see why their kids are so happy to come to school. Never happened before."

It was an hour before the haunted house. My classroom was rearranged into a chaotic maze of craft supplies. Desks were overturned, covered in paper, and corralled into a tunnel. Spider webs hung floor to ceiling, red paper covered the lights, and little rubber mice and bats lurked in the corners. We were ready.

The intercom clicked on: bomb drill time. My students let out a riotous groan of disappointment. Determined to prove I could handle this new impediment to our authentic learning experience, I sternly urged students to be quiet and to evacuate the building quickly. We walked south across the back of the school towards the designated safety site. There was no path. We marched across the scraggly high desert, sagebrush and prickly pear clinging to the pale rust soil. Students tripped over the bushes, trying to keep their costumes safe as they hurried past cacti. The wind picked up, sending swirls of sand into our eyes. A whirl of tumbleweed bounced against a second grader, sticking to the side of him.

My students started to giggle, but I barked at them to be quiet. A few seemed to lag behind. The sooner we completed the drill, the sooner we could start the haunted house. Why were they wasting time?

I turned back to look for the missing boys. They stood twenty yards away, and to my shock, each held a chubby, floppy-eared puppy. I was confused. Where had the puppies come from? A bright bolt of anger flashed through my head. We did not have time for this, whatever it was.

"Boys! What are you doing? This isn't the time to play with

puppies!" I shouted.

"Miss Hall," Tyson's voice rose above the wind, "They're my puppies! They must have followed me to school."

"We're rescuing them," Levi called.

"Yeah, we don't want them to blow up!" Jesus added.

The boys walked toward me, cradling their wriggling puppies. One licked the corn syrup blood from Jesus' fingers. The boys laughed, pure gold threads rising out into the chaotic afternoon. I stopped mid-stride, speechless. It sounded like joy.

I stared at them. Three boys, fake blood smeared across their faces, vampire capes whipping in the wind, stared back with bright, sparkling eyes. They looked happy. How could that be? Everything had gone wrong. Instead of having the long-awaited haunted house, we trudged through the desert to practiced bomb evacuations. This was the biggest disaster of my brief teaching career. But here the boys stood, grinning with wide, wild smiles, snuggling puppies in their arms. They don't just look happy, I realized. They looked like this may have been their best afternoon ever at school.

"That's a good idea to rescue the puppies," I said slowly. "Thank you."

"We're not in trouble?"

I looked back at the line of my students, now far in the distance. "Not unless you can't catch up with the class before the principal sees you. Think you can run and carry the puppies at the same time?"

They nodded, giggling. We took off together, running through the brush to the waiting group.

We repeated the bomb drill procedure two more times. Amazingly, we still had time for our Halloween celebration. Inside the haunted house, my students gleefully screeched and wailed under desks, tugged at visitors' sleeves, and held out jello "brains." Jesus dramatically gulped the corn syrup blood, then screamed and crashed to the floor in a death heap. The visitors were wild with excitement. They hugged each other, trembled, or showed bravado with scoffing laughter. We heard classes outside whooping with joy. "This is the most fun *ever*!" a second grader gleefully shouted. It was the first time I had seen so many happy kids at school, other than the last day.

When my students walked out of the classroom at dismissal,

buzzing on fruit punch, candy, and praise, they radiated satisfaction and pride. The assistant principal stopped several on their way to the busses.

"So," he said gruffly, "this was your big 'learning project.' What did you learn?"

"Candy in school is awesome!" Devon screeched.

Brynn, one of the few girls in the class, gave him a look. "We learned that we can make something big and special for the whole school," she said primly.

Tyson moved close to her. He had a particularly strained relationship with the assistant principal, owing to a recent fistfight on the playground, supposedly about the honor of his mother.

"Yeah, she's right. We did something special for everyone." His voice grew louder. "That means ... we aren't as bad as everyone says we are." With that, they turned and walked to the door. Each seemed a little taller than they had when they arrived that morning. My heart radiated pride.

Barb clapped a hand on my shoulder, interrupting my thoughts. "Fabulous day. Will you please do this again next year?"

"Maybe," I laughed. "It depends if fake blood comes out of the carpet."

***

In the end, there was no second haunted house. The next Halloween, I was teaching in a school thousands of miles away. My mother had cancer; I moved back home. My new school had Halloween traditions, like as a costume parade and class parties organized by eager parent volunteers. It was as far away from our wild and scrappy Halloween as I could imagine. It was also bittersweet. I missed my first students fiercely, painfully. I felt like I had betrayed them when I left. I did the only thing I could think of to honor them: I held tight to the lessons they taught me that Halloween.

In my classroom now, laughter is essential. I know some of the best moments are the least planned. Learning objectives are important, of course, but they must be balanced with the joy of being a child. And when that joy arrives, stomping like the hooves of wild animals, we must open the door and let it in. Childhood is short; memories are long.

When joy arrives in my classroom, I think of the boys standing in the high desert, puppies clutched to their chests, and I let it in.

Danielle Hall teaches sixth grade and supervises student teachers at the Smith College Campus School in Northampton, Massachusetts. An elementary educator for the past eleven years, she started teaching on the eastern edge of the Navajo Reservation in New Mexico. Since then, she has taught in a one-room schoolhouse off the coast of Maine, a progressive private school in Pennsylvania, and a public school in Topsham, Maine. She earned her B.A. in studio art from Wellesley College and her masters in elementary education from Smith College. She is a teacher consultant for the Southern Maine Writing Project. In her free time, Danielle can be found on a trapeze in western Massachusetts.

Trespassing and Transgressing: Opening the Door and Outing My Practice

Susan R. Adams

"When one door closes another door opens; but we so often look so long and so regretfully upon the closed door, that we do not see the ones which open for us."
—*Alexander Graham Bell*

When I was launched as a young teacher in 1985, my fledgling wings were barely strong enough to keep me aloft as I competed for scarce jobs, resorting to substitute teaching and maternity leave positions while I waited for someone to die or to retire. When I finally got my first "real" teaching position two years later, my first task as a professional teacher was to scrape the spit wads off the walls and pitch out twenty-five year old textbooks left behind in the filthy classroom I inherited from its previous occupant. It was nothing fancy: four cinderblock walls, the few posters I owned, a battle scarred desk, a teacher chair that snagged all my nylons, a bank of windows that leaked and a door, but it was mine, all mine. Nothing gave me more pleasure than unlocking the door to my classroom and surveying my little kingdom every morning.

Much has been made of teachers closing their classroom doors and basically doing whatever they like, regardless of what other teachers were doing. I must confess that closing my door was what I had been trained implicitly and explicitly to do by my mentors and my teacher education program. The door marked the edge of my kingdom, the limit of my authority, and the barrier which shielded my kingdom from outside invaders and witnesses. I controlled who entered and who exited at all times. It is amazing to me now that I was trusted to know what to do, what to teach, how to teach it and how to handle the 155 hormone-riddled adolescents I saw each day. I was determined to demonstrate my ability to maintain and strengthen my little kingdom and thus I hoped to earn the respect of my colleagues and administrators.

So each period, I closed the door and did the best I could to enlighten, entertain, and educate my students as they struggled to learn to speak Spanish. Except for my students, no one really knew what I was doing from day to day. As long as I turned in grades and attendance on time, kept the noise down, and didn't fail too many star athletes, no one challenged my curriculum or my methods. Frankly, I was relieved that no one asked because I would have been hard pressed to explain or justify my curricular decisions beyond blindly following a textbook and occasionally breaking the monotony of the textbook by memorizing poems, attempting a bit of journal writing, and writing dialogs in Spanish. Basically I was replicating what I had experienced myself as a student, but in ways I hoped were more innovative and fresh than what my teachers had done.

I continued in this way for several years, but, over time, a creeping paranoia began to whisper in my mind. *Was I an effective teacher? Were my students really learning?* World language standards emerged on the scene, but, thankfully, they only seemed to confirm what I was already doing, rather than challenge my thinking. I began to notice now that I closed the door as a way of protecting myself and my curriculum from scrutiny.

Rather abruptly, I shifted from teaching Spanish to teaching English as Second Language (ESL) at a new school. Suddenly, none of my old methods, standbys and habits seemed to work at all. I floundered my way through those first days and hoped that no one in this new school would notice that I was ingloriously starting from scratch after fifteen years of teaching Spanish. Hiding my uncertainty would have been much easier if I could have just shut the door as usual, but this classroom had multiple entrances; teachers, librarians, and administrators routinely cut through my classroom space located in an annex behind the library. Two paraprofessionals used space in the corners to work with students. Meetings, videotaping, and events were held on the other side of a heavy accordion curtain. Suddenly, I felt like my practice was on public display, my teaching a performance for anyone and everyone to see. In vain, I repeatedly and firmly shut the door, but still the traffic in and out continued unabated. I finally had to relinquish control and get comfortable with adults observing my every move.

Gradually I learned to relax and to not only tolerate the traffic, but use the interruptions as opportunities to showcase the work of my students and to build strong working relationships with my colleagues. Teachers were intrigued by what we were doing in this ESL classroom, noticing that my ESL students were visibly more at ease here than they were in mainstream classrooms. Conversations bubbled up, and my colleagues began seeking my advice and insights into helping my ESL students navigate high school. I shared project ideas and approaches and in return got helpful feedback and encouragement from other teachers. Administrators began asking me to take the lead on reform efforts and to represent the building at district meetings.

As my practice became more visible, I began to realize how restrictive privacy had been to my own learning and how liberating it was to publicize my work. I felt more confident of my skills and abilities than ever before, and I began to truly enjoy working with my colleagues. Instead of fearing discovery, now I was free to laugh, shake my head wonderingly, and say, "Wow, this idea just did not work!" and invite teachers and even students to help me rethink my approach.

Now my work is teaching graduate courses for practicing teachers, and there is simply no way for me to close the door. Every instructional decision I make is noticed, challenged, questioned and critiqued by sixty-five professional teachers every week. It is tempting to revert to my old default position and close the door. This level of scrutiny is exhausting, but transparency in my practice is how I earn the right to push each of them to open their doors and share their practice with their colleagues. I am encouraged and strengthened by the words of bell hooks[9]:

> Educators are compelled to confront the biases that
> have shaped teaching practices in our society and to
> create new ways of knowing, different strategies for
> the sharing of knowledge...[to] celebrate teaching
> that enables transgressions-a movement against and
> beyond boundaries.

Opening the door is a transgressive act, a sort of trespassing into space that was previously private property, but we deny ourselves the opportunity to enrich our practice and to reignite our own passion for learning when we remain safely behind closed doors. What have I missed while my door was closed? What did my students lose because I was too fearful to learn from them and from my colleagues? Now not only is my door open, but my heart and mind are open to the new possibilities teachers create when we bring our practice into the light.

Susan R. Adams was most recently the Project Alianza Director in the College of Education at Butler University where she now teaches ESL courses for pre-service and practicing teachers. A former high school Spanish and ESL teacher and instructional coach, Susan is a doctoral candidate in Literacy, Culture, and Language in Education at Indiana University at the School of Education in Indianapolis. She is a national facilitator and Critical Friends group coach, a teacher consultant with the National Writing Project, and a site leader of the Hoosier Writing Project. Her research interests include equity, teacher transformation, and ELL student writing development.

You Can't Tell by Looking

Laurie Thurston

I'd lost count the number of times my student teacher wiped away tears. Each morning during our prep, she struggled to modify lesson plans crafted the night before that she hoped and prayed would engage our fourth period freshmen English II class. You've all had this class: nearly half are repeating, every other student is labeled academic priority and has a 504 or an IEP, and more than seventy-five percent of them qualify for free and reduced lunch. The class where any one person absent or present or late or whatever can tip the entire precarious balance; the class that wakes you up at two in the morning in a cold sweat. You know this class.

So, imagine trying to instruct a student teacher, one who comes from a very different world than these kids before her, on how to create a safe space for learning and trust, how to model risk taking and reaching kids where they are in order to take them where they need to go.

***

"I wish someone would have told me it would be a long trimester."

Thing is, I had no idea how true that statement would become. In the span of ten weeks, from mid-March through June, four people close to many of our students lost their lives to violence. Four people. Dead. Two of these victims were only fourteen years old. One, a girl who was shot by her estranged boyfriend and is still missing; another, a boy who was gunned down in a public park while two of my students stood beside him. How could you concentrate on a novel when you've just returned from a vigil praying to learn where your friend's body was hidden? Why would you care about subject-verb agreement when you've witnessed your friend get shot in the head not a foot from you?

Barely halfway through this tumultuous trimester, I'd watched the grammar unit crash and burn and, now, I was bearing witness to a novel unit spiraling toward the same fiery fate. More than three-fourths of the class was failing; a couple students had been suspended; my student teacher was losing sleep; I'd run out of Kleenex. But this wasn't about her, not really. In teaching, there are far more variables out of your control than in. Anyone in front of a classroom knows this. But, I also wasn't doing my job; I wasn't meeting my student teacher where *she* was, wasn't creating a safe place for her to take risks and trust. I was not modeling how to help navigate a class through school while also helping navigate them through grieving and loss. Unfortunately (or fortunately, depending upon your point of view), I'd had experience—too much experience—helping my New York students through the grieving process. I knew what needed to be done, so it was time to reclaim our period four class here in Portland, Oregon.

In my classroom back in New York, I had a poster taped to my desk that read, *"If we don't model what we teach, we are teaching something else."* And whenever something goes wrong, feels "off," or isn't as effective as I think it should have been, I go back to that statement and look at what I did or did not do. And what I needed to do now was model for her how to resuscitate a class that had collapsed as a community. This wasn't something I could help her tweak in a lesson plan; it was about showing her how to break out of her comfort zone and be vulnerable with a group of young people who were scared, hurt, angry, and confused. It was about demonstrating how to maintain high expectations and a learning environment while giving the space to reflect and share and begin healing.

***

"You can't tell by looking…"

I tell all new teachers, "There's a *why* behind the *what*." Disruptive students aren't simply trying to make your life miserable; they're really not. The goal is to discover the "why" and create classroom opportunities to allow students to learn to manage themselves. Now, I can *say* this to my student teacher, and I did. Often. But, just as with young people, this needed to be shown, modeled, practiced to be truly understood.

So I came up with a plan. As a class and as individuals, we were going to explore the concept of a Firewalk: the notion that all of us have, or will one day have, an experience that will challenge us to our core, to force us to discover who we truly are. Some of us "walk fire" with others, as in the story I shared of my youngest sister's battle with cancer; other times, we "walk fire" on our own, as I did with the unexpected death of my middle sister. Since many of the students in this class were so deeply affected by the losses they'd recently experienced, I wanted to provide them an outlet to tell, write and illustrate stories in a 'zine format, choosing two pages to submit to a class publication of shared work. But I needed to first model—for them—what it meant to take risks, to publicly share personal thinking and writing.

After three days of reflecting, goal setting and class community building activities, they were ready. We were ready. I was ready. To create the safe space needed, we rearranged ourselves in a circle so that everyone could be seen, no one would be allowed to leave the space once the story sharing began and the person holding the Magic Ball was the only one allowed to speak. I'd introduced this purple glitter-filled rubber ball earlier in the year for just this purpose. Used only for class meetings and truly serious matters, it symbolized importance and set the tone I needed now.

I rolled the ball between my palms and began, "I've not told this story to any of you before so I'm not sure what will happen as I begin to tell it now. It's the hardest event I've ever had to navigate in my life." Placing the ball in front of me, I opened a two-year-old journal and began to read, "You can't tell by looking that, one week ago, I received a phone call from home that would forever change the way I live my life…" And I continued with the story of losing my sister Cheryl, who was profoundly mentally retarded, due to the neglectful act of her caregiver. I shared how it felt to give permission to remove her from life support, to be 3,000 miles away from any family or friend who knew me personally, to have to testify in court about that horrid night, to have to help my mother deal with the loss of her child.

My students listened in a way I'd never seen before. Not one extraneous sound, not one inappropriate comment or reaction. Just a supportive space for me to share my Firewalk. And the next day? My student teacher shared her story. Admittedly, she was very nervous, and I reminded her that she did not need to share if that made her uncomfortable, but I added that if she was going to ask her students to take risks and be vulnerable, she had to be willing to do the same.

And she did.

She shared with the students the story of her brother and then gave them a copy of a letter she'd written to a judge, asking him for leniency in his sentencing. The students read this letter with a focus and intensity I hadn't seen the entire trimester; they listened to her speak about her father's drug addiction, and I saw in their eyes compassion and an emerging connection. They nodded their heads when she talked about immersing herself in school and books as her escape, while her brother turned to crime and drugs for his. It was clearly not easy for her, to tell this personal story, to take off the mask and reveal true vulnerability. Yet, when she'd finished, one of the students said, "We had no idea. You seemed so perfect, like you'd had this ideal life." And she seemed genuinely shocked they thought this, but recovered by repeating the writing prompt from the day before, "You can't tell by looking."

A waterfall of stories flooded the circle over the next two weeks: hospitalization for failure to thrive, witness to domestic violence, drug addiction, sexual abuse, rape, the incarceration of siblings and parents, the death of family members, murder of friends, homelessness, suicide attempts... Later in the day, my student teacher reached for yet another Kleenex. "I had no idea. No wonder," she shook her head. "Now I understand: what you meant by the why behind the what." But not all the stories were tragic, several students felt a sense of guilt for not having experienced such trauma. They had come to me after class or during lunch to whisper, "I don't have a Firewalk, what should I do?" And I'd told them to create a 'zine that reflected who they were and what influences helped them become that person. So, in addition to the pain, our class also got to hear stories of sports and work and immigration and church and family and the desire to go to college. Many of these students began their stories by thanking the others who shared such powerfully personal struggles. And, by the close of the unit, several students—even those who'd shown palpable animosity earlier in the trimester—were now talking, nodding hello, and sitting next to each other.

***

"What does it mean to be a community?"

On the final day, after the bound magazines of chosen pages were handed out and read, we stood to share our appreciations. Many thanked the student teacher for not giving up on them, for sharing her story, for trusting them. They thanked each other for being real and listening and not judging. Then others thanked me for bringing us all together again as a community and letting every voice be heard.

I could not have told my student teacher how to teach this unit because it was the first time I'd taught it. Even after actually facilitating such an experience, it remains a challenge to put into words exactly what I did, what *we* did. But that's precisely why I think teaching is so often miraculous. It necessitates being present, listening, truly hearing what is both said and—more often—not said, so that what is needed can be uncovered and shared. It's about nurturing acceptance, modeling understanding, and insisting on excellence.

Teaching is not about curriculum. It's about kids, about community.

Teaching is our Firewalk.

Laurie Thurston taught English/language arts within a Rochester, New York program for "disengaged" high school students that she developed and directed. In addition to her seventeen years in the classroom, she spent two years as an instructional leadership coach for the Oregon Small School Initiative, which worked to sustain the development of small schools across the state. She's presented at several conferences sharing best practices and strategies for teaching reluctant readers and writers, including the New York State Alternative Network Association, the National Council for Teacher Educators, the Oregon Association of Teacher Educators, and the National Association for Multicultural Education. She penned a regular column regarding teaching in the *Alternative Network Journal* and has published several other articles about teaching and writing. In addition to teaching humanities at LEP Charter High School in Portland, she's been an adjunct in the M.A.T. program at Marylhurst University where she teaches pre-service teachers about writing and literacy across content areas.

❖ Postscript ❖

Sacrifice

Marni Valerio

I have a confession to make: I did not want to write this. I walked away from fulltime teaching, and I guiltily read every essay in this book through the lens of my perceived failure. Until one day, as Dan and I were driving and discussing the immense burdens of teaching, I admitted out loud that I had sacrificed my teaching for my family. Suddenly, I no longer felt unworthy to write. My story fit. For a hardworking teacher, the burdens of teaching are immeasurable. There are rewards but not necessarily for my own family. Oh, and he quickly reminded me that I was still teaching.

As a secondary teacher, I dressed up. Not in fancy clothing, but rather as a pirate, a conductor, a judge, Madame Geoffrin. I remember sitting in a post-evaluation meeting with a former assistant principal in 1999. This man complimented my intellect and rapport with students, but he was concerned that I might burn out too early in my teaching career. He likened me to James Brown, the godfather of soul. My first thought went to my hair and wardrobe, but he continued saying he was afraid he would have to carry me out at the end of each teaching day. He thought I gave too much; he thought I should slow down and use a few more worksheets. I sat there dumbfounded, disillusioned because my supervisor would rather me do less. He would rather me be lackluster and lengthen my career than teach with energy until I no longer could. I ignored his advice.

Many years have passed, and I have yet to come to a college classroom in costume, but my teaching spirit remains intact. I still do not sit when I teach; I still dance at times when fostering discussion; I still believe that I am making a difference, and I aim to be constructive, energetic, and positive. My standards have not changed, but time, education, and parenting have taught me to listen more closely, to collaborate more fully, to share my own writing vulnerabilities, and to slow down when needed.

For me, teaching is really about empowerment and that does not change whether I am teaching seventh-grade Texas history, AP United States history, or composition at my local community college. Recently, we had the gift of a sixty-five degree day in January in Nebraska. I had the ability to meet my children and their friends and walk them home. I overheard my fifth-grade daughter tell the group that her teacher did not make them wear coats for recess. The teacher had said, "They were old enough to know if they were cold." As I listened, I marveled at this gift her teacher gave. She chose not to control; she empowered them with choice. That is all I can ask of a teacher of my own children: give them agency to choose, and, if they can choose the small things, they practice for the larger issues and decisions that will surely come their way. A day later, as I sat in the school workroom, her teacher came in, and I said thank you for that small kindness. This is just one example of the thousands of minuscule lessons educators teach with grace and compassion; teachers need to know the difference they make in the life of a child.

For many, the idea of a teacher perplexes. Admittedly, each of us has experienced horror at the hands of an evil instructor. Alternately, most of us remember a teacher's extreme kindness, patience, or encouragement. American culture trends toward caricature, towards labels. Teachers must be this "sort" or that "type." However, as a reader of this book soon realizes, oversimplifications do not apply. Teachers are individuals who serve other individuals. The essays in this collection highlight this individuality and the unique approaches and sacrifices of people who teach.

I am grateful to have read all the essays that were submitted for this collection. I commend the people brave enough to share their intimate writing. They know what they do, how hard they try, and how heavy the work seems. They know what teaching means.

❖ Notes ❖

Amanda Marek's *Teaching Spanish and Learning Latino*

1. Hispanic indicates a person from a Spanish speaking background, including Spain and Latin America. Latino indicates a person from Latin America and includes non-Spanish speaking people and countries, such as Brazil. Since my students are all Spanish speaking and one is from Spain, I use the term Hispanic to describe them. Most of the culture I encountered through them is Latino.

Laurie Zum Hofe's *Articulating the Blur*

2. Lunsford, Andrea and Lisa Ede. "Crimes of Reading and Writing." *Teaching Rhetorica: Theory, Pedagogy, Practice.* Ed. Kate Ronald and Joy Ritchie. Portsmouth, NH: Boynton/Cook, 2006.

3. Newkirk, Thomas. *The Performance of Self in Student Writing.* Portsmouth, NH: Boynton/Cook, 1997.

Kurt Reynold's *The Myth of a Teacher*

4. Camus, Albert. "The Myth of Sisyphus." *Themes in World Literature.* Eds. George P. Elliott, Philip McFarland, Harvey Granite & Morse Peckham. Boston: Houghton Mifflin Co., 1975. 229-232.

Susan Martens' *Eight Stories about Teaching I Never Told You*

5. This story appears in Pen Campbell and Dan Holt's excellent article, "Episodic Fiction: Another Way to Tell a Story," originally published in the Summer 2001 issue of *The Quarterly of the National Writing Project (Vol. 23*, No. 3). It is available online at nwp.org and in the book *Breakthroughs: Classroom Discoveries about Teaching Writing*, edited by Amy Bauman and Art Peterson and published by the National Writing Project in 2002.

Joel Shatsky *Reflections of an "Easy Grader"*

6. See his"Grading: The Issue Is Not How But Why" *Educational Leadership* from October 1994

7. See *http://www.ncpublicschools.org/docs/data/reports/dschday.pdf*

Kelly Norris' *Teaching To Kill a Mockingbird*

8. *www.anti-racismonline.com*

Susan Adams' *Trespassing and Transgressing: Opening the Door and Outing My Practice*

9. hooks, bell. *Teaching to Transgress: Education as the Practice of Freedom.* London: Routledge, 1994. p. 12.

❖ The Editors ❖

Daniel Boster is in his fifteenth year as a high school English teacher. He has a B.A. in English and philosophy from the University of Texas, an M.A. in English from the University of Wisconsin-Eau Claire, and is now working on a Ph.D. in rhetoric and composition at the University of Nebraska-Lincoln. He teaches at Ralston High School in Omaha, Nebraska, where he also teaches occasional college creative writing and literature courses. He is a co-director of the Nebraska Writing Project, and, in addition to his academic writing, is a poet. His work has appeared in, among others, *Trajectory*, *Cream City Review*, *Anderbo.com*, and *Hiram Poetry Review*.

Marni Valerio is currently an English instructor and writing center consultant at Metropolitan Community College in Omaha. For many years, she taught middle and high school social studies in Texas, Wisconsin, and Nebraska and, later, composition and literature at the University of Nebraska-Omaha and Creighton University. Marni has a B.A. in history from the University of Dallas and an M.A. in English from the University of Nebraska-Omaha. Her thesis is a creative nonfiction collection, entitled *Cleaning Out*.

Daniel and Marni are married and live in midtown Omaha with their children, Libby and Noble.

❖ Acknowledgements ❖

Words can't quite express the gratitude we feel for Jeff Lacey and Calvin Banks of Rogue Faculty Press and their unwavering dedication to this project from the beginning.

Of course, there wouldn't be a book without all of the people who shared their stories. Working with them has been an amazing experience and convinced us, once again, that, yes, actual teachers are the people best suited to write about education and teaching.

A "shout out" to the students, teachers, and administrators of Lancaster High School and De Soto Junior High School in Texas; Dominican High School and Wauwatosa West High School in Wisconsin; Louisville High School, Mercy High School, Ralston High School, and Metropolitan Community College in Nebraska; and Buena Vista University in Iowa for giving us opportunities to teach and witness great people and educators at work.

Thanks to Linda Christensen, Penny Kittle, Dr. Margaret Macintyre Latta, Dr. Marilyn Valerio, and Dr. George White for supporting this project by being our first readers.

It probably wouldn't have occurred to us to attempt this if it wasn't for all of the incredible teachers of the National Writing Project and the Nebraska Writing Project, especially Dr. Robert Brooke of the University of Nebraska-Lincoln, who constantly advocates for the idea that teachers are the experts.

Thanks to our families and friends for their faithful encouragement.

Finally, to Libby and Noble, we want to say thanks for letting us sit at our computers so much during the past year. We'll now have more time to play catch, watch *Harry Potter* movies, play four square, and go for walks. We promise.

Made in the USA
Columbia, SC
08 January 2020